Man
As God Intended

*A Theological Survey
from an
Anthropological Perspective*

James A. Fowler

C.I.Y. PUBLISHING
P.O. BOX 1822
FALLBROOK, CALIFORNIA 92088-1822
http://www.Christinyou.net

MAN AS GOD INTENDED

*A Theological Survey
from an Anthropological Perspective*

Published by C.I.Y. Publishing
P.O. Box 1822
Fallbrook, California 92088-1822

Printed in the United States of America

13 digit ISBN – 978-1-929541-28-7

Cataloging-in-Publication Data

Fowler, James A.
Man as God Intended: *A Theological Survey from an Anthropological Perspective.*
1. Theology, Doctrine of Man
2. Anthropology, Theological
2. Man – Doctrine of
I.   Title

Dedication

With the utmost of gratitude, I dedicate this volume to several men who were instrumental in the formation of the thoughts herein. What these men shared became the springboards for the formulation of my own thinking and teaching.

Major W. Ian Thomas has been my foremost spiritual mentor. One week after I was regenerated and began to understand spiritual realities in 1973, Jim Morris of the Navigators handed me Major Thomas' book, *The Saving Life of Christ*. Soon thereafter I read *The Mystery of Godliness* which was even better suited to my theological mind. In fact, the title and theme of this book is a phrase that I borrowed from the teaching of Major Thomas.

The three pastoral colleagues who were used of God to reveal my spiritual bankruptcy and the need for spiritual regeneration were also vessels used of God to assist in the formation of my life and thought from 1973 to 1981. Pastors Harry Jennings, Frank Miller and Vernon Whitmore essentially discipled me for almost eight years as we prayed together, studied together, and played golf together. It was Harry Jennings who first encouraged me to put these studies in written form, and I am sure he is rejoicing in heaven as they are now being disseminated in this book.

James A. Fowler
2005

Acknowledgements

I want to acknowledge and recognize

. . . the various audiences, in churches, seminars, retreats, Bible schools and seminaries, who have graciously listened to these messages over the past thirty years. Your response, questions and challenges have been beneficial in the development and refinement of my thinking and teaching,

. . . the participants of the Neighborhood Church who have listened to these themes for twenty-four years,

. . . my sister, Sylvia Burnett, for editing assistance,

. . . Kathie Larsen for a final edit and checking of scripture references,

. . . and my dear wife, Gracie, who has often chided me for going into "screen-saver" mode as I pondered these spiritual realities.

Table of Contents

Foreword i

1   What is Man? 1

2   The Constitution of Man 11

3   The Fall of Man 23

4   The Natural Man 41

5   The Perfect Man 63

6   The Restoration of Man 81

7   The Response of Man 113

8   The Regeneration of Man 135

9   The Fullness of God in Man 153

10 The Sanctification of Man 181

11 The Responsibility of Man 191

12 The End of Man 205

Endnotes 217
Glossary of Terms 223

Foreword

Caution must be exercised in approaching theological studies from an anthropological perspective. One must never elevate the creature, man, above the Creator, God. The proper starting point of theology must always be the Being and character of God. Acting out of His own Being, always consistent with His character, God created all things, and man was the highest life-form of the created order of this physical world. Much of theology, therefore, pertains to the interactions of God and mankind. The redemptive acts of God, in His Son Jesus Christ, are even more specifically related to mankind in the Self-revelation of God in His Son, whereby the "Word became flesh" (John 1:14), and the "man Christ Jesus" (I Tim. 2:5) engaged Himself to redeem and restore humanity. So, although our stated subject matter is "man," humanity is not our focal point, but we focus on God in Christ and His divine activity with man, in order that "man might be man as God intended man to be." (The phrase is not original with the author, but must be credited to British Bible teacher, Major W. Ian Thomas, from whose teaching the author has greatly benefited.)

In this age of gender sensitivities, a word of explanation is probably necessary concerning the use of "man" throughout this book. "Man," as used in the title and elsewhere in the text, is a generic reference to mankind or humanity. Although brief mention will be made to the sexual division of humanity into male and female genders, the predominance of our theological concern transcends gender specificity. Whether male or female, we are part of the generic classification of mankind, who are "made one in Christ Jesus" (Gal. 3:28). In addition, let it be noted that pronominal references to the human race will retain the traditional masculine gender (i.e. "he," "his," "him") with no intended slight or denigration of the female gender.

This volume is not intended to be a technical treatise of academic theology, so technical terminology has been kept to a minimum – utilized only where precision of explanation is facilitated by such use. For the most part general biblical and theological vocabulary has been employed that should be understandable to the average Christian reader. (Readers of the first printing, however, continued to request a "glossary of terms," so this has been added to this printing, attempting to define and explain some terms utilized in this book.)

These studies have been taught in various forms and forums over the past thirty years – in churches, retreats, seminars, Bible schools and seminaries – in the United States, Canada, India, Indonesia, New Zealand, Philippines, etc. They are foundational to everything else that I teach and write. I often refer to this series as my "life message." It is my desire and hope that this volume may serve to enhance a clearer understanding of what God has done in Jesus Christ to allow "man to be *man as God intended*."

James A. Fowler
2005

1

What is Man?

The first man who ever lived, in conjunction with all mankind after him, must have pondered his own existence, asking the question, "What is man?" Every generation of mankind and every individual human being questions to some extent their meaning and purpose in the vast and perplexing context of the world around them. They ask questions like: "What am I?" "Who am I?" "Why am I? "How am I to function?" These are basic and fundamental questions which are not always easy to answer.

In what is perhaps some of the earliest of Hebrew literature, Job pondered just such a question. Not understanding the trials of life that he was suffering, Job asked God, "What is man that Thou dost magnify him, and that Thou art concerned about him; that Thou dost examine him every morning, and try him every moment?" (Job 7:17,18). Job was questioning the meaning of man's existence within the context of God's ultimate purposes.

The Psalmist asks a similar question concerning man's place in the created universe. "When I consider Thy heavens, the work of Thy fingers, the moon and the stars, which Thou hast ordained; What is man, that Thou dost take thought of him? And the son of man, that Thou dost care for him? Yet

Thou hast made him a little lower than God, and dost crown him with glory and majesty!" (Psalm 8:3-5). Again, when facing the hardships of conflicts and battles, the Psalmist, David, inquires, "O Lord, what is man, that Thou dost take knowledge of him? Or the son of man, that Thou dost think of him? Man is like a mere breath; His days are like a passing shadow" (Psalm 144:3,4).

These are human cries for the understanding of man's place and purpose within God's created order. They are legitimate questions which men should rightfully ponder in order to ascertain the purpose for which they were created.

In considering an answer to the question, "What is man?", we want to avoid the two extremes: We do not want to posit to man more than he is, nor do we want to relegate man to less than he is.

Man is not God. He does not become God, nor does he become "a god." The deification of humanity posits to mankind a potential that he does not possess, and can never live up to.

On the other hand, man is more than a mere animal. Though he may share physiological and behavioral characteristics with some animals, such as feeding, bleeding and breeding, the human being is constitutionally more advanced than an animal, and has a destiny that is not available to the animal kingdom.

To properly understand man's place and purpose, one must consider man in juxtaposition with God. The Creator, God, created the creature, man, to function in a particular relationship with Himself. If we can get a glimpse of how God functions, then perhaps we can begin to understand how man is intended to function.

God is independent, autonomous and self-generative. There is no one outside of God who in any way influences

2

His Being or His action. God is never dependent or contingent on anything or anyone else, nor does He derive what He is or does from anything or anyone outside of Himself. He is His own center of reference. He is self-existent, uncreated and eternal.

What God is, only God is! His attributes are exclusive to Himself and non-transferable. Only God is God! If we attempt to attribute to something or someone else, that which is exclusively an attribute of God, then we ever so subtly and inadvertently ascribe deity to that object. There is only one God. God is exclusively God, both in His Being and in His activity. He *does* what He *does*, because He *is* Who He *is*! God's primary function is to act as the God that He is. He never acts "out of character," for His activity is always in accord with His character, who He is! God acts as the independent, autonomous and self-generative God that He is, consistently expressing every facet of His character. God's primary function is **activity** that independently, autonomously and self-generatively expresses His own character.

How then does man function? There are some who would try to explain that man functions in the same way that we have just described God's function. The philosophical premise of humanism posits that man is his own center of reference. Humanism postulates that every human being is independent, autonomous and self-generative, with the inherent potentiality to be the cause of his own effects and the source of his own activity. Man is said to be "the master of his own fate." "He can chart his own course, run his own show, do his own thing, solve his own problems and control his own destiny." "If he can just perfect his intellect through advanced education and generate enough resources to effect his best efforts, man can improve himself and his environment to create a utopian 'heaven on earth'." "The potential of the independent human "self" is unlimited." "You can be anything you want to be." "You can achieve anything you set your mind to." These are the positivistic platitudes of humanistic thinking.

This independent self-potential premise pervades the thinking of Western society today. Assuming the sovereign self-generative capability of man, we are told, "You can do it!" From the time of our childhood we are read such books as *The Little Train That Could*, wherein the little train activates his best self-effort, saying "I think I can...I think I can...I think I can"...and he did it! This sets us up for the continued positing of ourselves via "positive thinking" and "possibility thinking" techniques. "Think yourself to the activating of your own success." "Will yourself to the top of the heap." And if perchance you do not make it, then seek out one of the self-help programs to better teach yourself how to achieve this success, or check yourself into a self-help clinic.

The assumption that man is an independent and autonomous being, capable of generating his own activity, is a deification of humanity. It postulates that man is his own god, individually and collectively. Using the superior intellectual reasoning of the human mind and the sovereign will to determine his own destiny, man can allegedly fulfill higher and higher levels of self-realization and create a heavenly utopia on earth. Why has this not happened over several millennia of the history of mankind? Who is to say that one man's reasoning is superior to another man's reasoning? This leads only to rationalistic relativism.

God alone is independent, autonomous and self-generating. As the divine Creator, He created man to be a creature who could only function by deriving all he is and does from spiritual resource. God did not create little "gods" and call them "human beings." The creature, man, was designed to

4

function only by constant contingency upon the Creator, God. In a dependent relationship upon God, man can allow God to express His character in the behavior of the man in ways that no other part of the created order is capable of, for man is the epitome of God's created order.

Man is dependent, contingent and derivative. He is not independent, autonomous and self-generating. If God's primary function is activity that independently and autonomously and self-generatively expresses His own character, then man's primary function is **receptivity** that dependently and contingently and derivatively allows God's activity to be expressed in the man.

The analogies that the Bible uses to describe the function of man usually describe the receptivity of man's function. Man is a recipient. He is pictured as a receptacle.

Writing to the Corinthians, Paul explains that Christians have the treasure of Christ Jesus "in earthen vessels, that the surpassing greatness of the power may be of God and not from ourselves" (II Cor. 4:7). The word for "vessels" usually referred to the old clay pots that were used as receptacles or containers of water, olive oil or wine. The container was not regarded as the object of value, but the value was in that which it contained. Paul indicates that Christian men and women are "vessels" which contain the ultimate "treasure" of the divine presence of Jesus Christ.

Man is also described as a "house" (II Cor. 5:1). A house is a dwelling-place for a personal occupant. The personal God is meant to inhabit the house of mankind. As He abides in our abode (John 15:4), we have the personal resource to function according to His intent.

Another analogy used to describe the receptivity of man is the image of a "temple." What is a temple? It is a structure that is meant to contain a god. Human beings are designed to receive and contain the presence of the living God within their spirit. Paul asks the Christians in Corinth, "Do you not know that your body is the temple of the Holy Spirit who is in you, whom you have from God, and that you are not your own?" (I Cor. 6:19). The living God intends to live and function within the temple of our body.

Man is a receiver, a recipient. Receptivity is the basis for all of man's function. We are faith-beings, designed for receptivity of God's activity, availability to God's ability.

In identifying man as a container or receptacle, it is important to note that man is obviously more than just an inanimate pot or pan, more than a non-living, impersonal clay jug. The Creator designed the creature, man, to be a personal choosing creature. In so doing, God self-limited his unlimited sovereign activity to correspond with the choices that man might make to depend upon Him and derive from Him in a personal faith-love relationship. Although only God has absolute free will to do anything He desires consistent with His character, and the power to accomplish such, He created man with freedom of choice, the volitional capability to choose and decide whether he would exercise such dependency and contingency upon his Maker. There was a freedom to accept or reject such a relationship of contingency upon the Creator. The rejection of such contingency upon God does not negate man's creaturely function of spiritual dependency and derivation however.

Man was solicited and seduced to make a choice to reject dependency upon the God who made him. The source of this solicitation came from a spirit-creature who had become the antithesis and antagonist of God. Lucifer, the light-bearer, within the ranks of the angelic host, was himself a creature, created by God, who was dependent, contingent and derivative. Exercising his freedom of choice, he made an apparently unsolicited decision to oppose God and to seek to be as God. The causation and reasoning for such is unrevealed and unknown to us. In so doing he became the fixed adversary of God, the Evil One, Satan, the devil. He is referred to as "the god of this world" (II Cor. 4:4), but this does not necessarily imply that he is independent, autonomous or self-generative. He is still derivative as he takes that which is of God and attempts to pervert it, distort it, misuse and abuse it. Thus he originates evil as the Evil One, and is the culpable cause of evil. The prime function of Satan is **negativity**. He takes that which is of God and attempts to negate the character and activity of God in the perversion, distortion and abortion of God's intent.

It was Satan in the form of a serpent who solicited man in the Garden of Eden (Gen. 3:1-5). As "the father of lies" (John 8:44), the Devil suggested to original man that he could "be like God" (Gen. 3:5). "You do not need God to be a man." "You can be a man apart from God." It was a false solicitation to freedom apart from dependency and contingency. It was the humanistic lie that man could be a self-oriented independent self with unlimited human potential to actualize himself in independent, autonomous and self-generative function. Impossible, for in so doing he would cease to be the contingent, derivative and dependent human creature that God created.

Why do evangelical Christians, even to this day, persist in declaring that when man rejected dependency upon God, he became independent? When original man listened to the solicitation of the Satanic tempter and disobeyed and sinned, the fall of man did not cause man to become independent, autonomous and self-generative. Man is still a dependent, contingent and derivative creature who became dependent upon Satan, "the spirit that works in the sons of disobedience" (Eph. 2:2). Fallen man is not able to self-generate anything. He cannot self-generate righteousness or unrighteousness, godliness or ungodliness, saintliness or sinfulness. "The one committing sin derives what he does from the devil" (I John 3:8). The fallen, natural man is contingent upon the "authority of Satan" (Acts 26:18), deriving what he does from "the prince of the power of the air" (Eph. 2:2), and deriving his identity as a "son of the devil" (I John 3:10) from the one on whom he is dependent. The natural man may think that he is independent and autonomous and free, but he is really a "slave to sin" (Rom. 6:6).

Evangelical Christians must beware of inadvertently falling into the humanistic premise. Mankind never functions independently, autonomously or self-generatively. Man is a spiritually dependent creature. "Not one of us lives of himself" (Rom. 14:7). "Not that we are adequate to consider anything as coming from ourselves, but our adequacy is of God" (II Cor. 3:5). We are contingent and dependent at every moment in time to derive our identity and our behavior from one spiritual source or the other, God or Satan. That is the way God created us as creatures.

Even within the context of evangelical teaching on the Christian life some teachers indicate that the alternative to living "by the Spirit" is to revert to an alleged self-generated personal resource, which they often call "self." A popular form of this teaching indicates that either Christ is on the throne of one's life or else "self" or "ego" is on the throne of one's life. Ever so subtly this teaching alleges that an independent self-resource takes effect whenever the Christian is not functioning under the Lordship of Jesus Christ. Satan disguises his activity under this cloak of "self" in order to deceive and destroy us. If we think that our problem is "self" or some "dirty old man" in us, then we begin to masochisti-

8

cally beat on ourselves and attempt to "die to self" in order to be better Christians. Contrary to such teaching, we do not become better Christians by crucifying or suppressing this alleged self-resource. We are indeed to "deny ourselves" (Luke 9:23) by disallowing the self-oriented selfishness that Satan inspires, but we do so by deriving all from Christ in faith. By exercising faithful receptivity of His activity we depend on Him to be the dynamic of His own demands, and remain contingent upon Christ for the expression of His life in our behavior unto the glory of God.

May we cease to even posit an independent personal resource of "self." It is the lie of humanism. We must reject *en toto* the idea that man can in any way be independent, autonomous or self-generative. In both his spiritual condition and his behavioral expression man is always a creature who is dependent, contingent and derivative. All that man is and does will be derived either from God or Satan.

God's intent, of course, is that His Spirit, the Spirit of Christ, might dwell in the spirit of a man who receives such by faith. Having received the presence of Christ by faith, we are to live by continued receptivity of His activity (Col. 2:6). The Christian life is a process of deriving all from Christ – His righteousness, His holiness, His wisdom, His love, His life lived out through us. "We have this treasure (Christ) in earthen vessels, that the surpassing greatness of the power may be of God, and not of ourselves" (II Cor. 4:7).

What is man? Man is a creature created by the Creator to function only by dependency and contingency upon a spiritual source. By personal freedom of choice he decides to derive his identity and behavior either from God or Satan. His nature, his character and his destiny will be thus derived by receptivity to one or the other. He will either be destroyed by

Satanic dysfunction or be saved by the restoration of God's function in the man by His Son, Jesus Christ.

2

The Constitution of Man

It is amazing how abysmally ignorant men have been about their own composition and capabilities. Only as we understand how a human being is constituted or formed will we then be able to understand how mankind was intended to function.

Our study of man's constitution or composition must begin in the first chapter of Genesis – the record of the creation of all things. In the creation account there seems to be a progression of increasingly complex levels of capacity for life-function. "In the beginning God created the heavens and the earth" (Gen. 1:1). The living God created non-living substance; the greater bringing the lesser into being. Later the living God commences to create forms which have the capacity for life in several categories. It would be quite illogical to posit that objects which have life could have been derived from a non-living source. The living is not derived from the non-living. Nehemiah explains that "God dost give life to all" that is living on the earth (Neh. 9:6).

Body

The first created form which had capacity for life was the plant kingdom. "God said, 'Let the earth sprout vegetation, plants yielding seed, fruit trees bearing fruit after their kind, with seed in them'" (Gen. 1:11). Plants have physical life in a physical form. The physical form wherein that physical life is expressed is referred to as a "body." The botanist, for example, refers to the "body" of the plant. Though the physical life within the plant is extremely complex in terms of the processes of nourishment, reproduction, photosynthesis, etc., there are obvious limitations to the expression of physical life within the plant kingdom behaviorally.

When the animal kingdom came into being, they also had physical life in a physical form referred to as a "body," but they also had an additional capacity for life-function that included behavioral capabilities. "God said, 'Let the waters teem with swarms of living creatures, and let birds fly above the earth in the open expanse of the heavens.' And God created the great sea monsters, and every living creature that moves..." (Gen. 1:20,21).

Soul

The capacity for behavioral life-function is referred to as "soul." Does an animal have this capacity of "soul" function? Many have been taught that an animal does not have soul, and that the distinguishing characteristic that differentiates man from an animal is that "man has a soul." What does the behavioral life-function of "soul" entail? Behavioral capability involves mental, emotional and volitional function. There is an ability to think with the mind, feel with the emotions, and determine with the will. To what extent do the different species of animals have the capacity to reason, feel and thus decide their course of action? Obviously this varies within the different species of animals; some have very limited behavioral capacity and others have quite complex behavioral capabilities.

The field of study that concerns itself with behavioral capability is that which is identified as "psychology." The word "psychology" is derived from two Greek words: *psuche* meaning "soul," and *logos* meaning "word" or "logic," which together refer to "the study of the soul." Most of the older psychology texts indicated this meaning in their introduction, but the meaning is inexplicably deleted from most modern texts, probably to avoid any correlation with "religion." The educational discipline of psychology considers thinking processes, emotive processes, and the decision-making processes that activate behavior; the way we think, the way we feel, and the way we decide to act, as well as the consequences thereof. But, the question might still be asked, "Do animals have this capacity?"

Throughout the New Testament the Greek word *psuche* is translated as "soul" or as the "life" function of the soul, which involves the individuality of the person, for it is in this capacity that differing personalities develop. Jesus said, for example, "whoever wishes to save his life (*psuche*) shall lose it; but whoever loses his life (*psuche*) for My sake shall find it. ...What will a man give in exchange for his soul (*psuche*)?" (Matt. 16:25,26).

When the Old Testament was translated from Hebrew into Greek in the Septuagint (LXX), the Greek word *psuche* was employed six hundred times to translate the Hebrew word *nephesh*, which likewise referred to the behavioral capacity of "soul." The very first usage of the Hebrew word *nephesh* appears in the verses cited above concerning the

13

introduction of animals into God's created order. Literally these verses read, "And God said, 'Let the waters swarm with swarmers having living soul (*nephesh*)...' And God created the great sea-monsters and all having a living soul (*nephesh*)" (Gen. 1:20,21)[1] Later in the same chapter of Genesis, God says, "Let the earth bring forth living soul (*nephesh*) after its kind, cattle and creepers, and the beasts of the earth after its kind" (Gen. 1:24).[2] Then again reference is made to "every beast of the earth, to every bird of the heavens, and to every creeper on the earth in which is a living soul (*nephesh*)" (Gen. 1:30).[3] Reiterating the creation of animals, the second chapter of Genesis records that "Jehovah God formed every beast of the field and every bird of the sky, and brought them to man to see what he would call them; and whatever the man called a living soul (*nephesh*), that was its name" (Gen. 2:19).[4] The same usage is found in Genesis 9: 10,15,16.

It is obvious from these verses that the Hebrew word *nephesh*, translated into English as "soul," is applied to animals. Zoologists have certainly demonstrated that animals have varying capabilities of determinative behavioral function within the diverse species. Chimpanzees, dogs, cats, and even insects have this behavioral capacity of life-function.

Spirit

What, then, makes man different from the animals? The human race has the capacity for physical life-function within a physical body, as do both plants and animals. With the animal kingdom we share the capacity for behavioral life-function within a soul that has mental, emotional and volitional operations, and the human capabilities for such exceed all known abilities within all the species of the animal kingdom. Man has greater capacity for reasoning, responding with emotion, and making complex decisions than does any animal. The progression of creation indicates that man not only has the capacity for physical life-function in a "body," and the capacity for behavioral life-function in a "soul," but to these are added the capacity for spiritual life-function in a "spirit." The prophet explains that "the Lord stretches out the heavens, lays the foundation of the earth, and forms the spirit of man within him" (Zech. 12:1). Job also indicates that "the Spirit of God has made me, and the breath of the Almighty gives me life" (Job 33:4), for "it is a spirit in man, and the breath of the Almighty gives them understanding" (Job 32:8). Man, the highest of God's creation, is designed by the Creator, the "God who is Spirit," to "worship Him in spirit and truth" (John 4:24). Anthropologists and sociologists explain that man has always been, and is always, a worshipping creature, which is never true within the animal kingdom. That which distinguishes man from the animals is that man has the additional capacity of spiritual life-function.

Mankind has the capacity for life-function at three levels: body and soul and spirit. The apostle Paul prayed for the Thessalonian Christians that "the God of peace Himself might sanctify them entirely; and their **spirit** (*pneuma*) and **soul** (*psuche*)and **body** (*soma*) might be preserved complete, without blame at the coming of the Lord Jesus Christ" (I Thess. 5:23). His desire was that Christians might be sanctified, might "be set apart to function as intended," at every level of their life-function, physical, psychological and spiritual. The conjunction "and" between each level of life-function sets each apart as distinct and important for God's intent in man. Many exegetes, expositors and teachers have failed to note the distinction of these three capacities of life-function. The failure to do so leads to much ambiguity and misunderstanding.

It must first be admitted that these are not three substantive "parts" of man, capable of being partitioned or compartmentalized. That is why we continue to refer to these as three levels of capacity for life-function, rather than entities which comprise man. The theological terms which refer to the tripartite or trichotomous nature of man are misleading, therefore, and are best avoided. The two-dimensional diagrams used to illustrate these varying life-functions are always inadequate since they picture separate compartments. (See diagram on page 22.)

Man's most cursory pondering of his own constitution yields a distinguishing of that which can be seen and that which cannot be seen, the visible and the invisible, the corporeal and the incorporeal. The body, being physical and material and tangible, is differentiated from the inner being of man, which is immaterial. Jesus explained that we should "not fear those who kill the body, but are unable to kill the soul (*psuche*); but rather fear Him who is able to destroy both soul (*psuche*) and body in hell" (Matt. 10:28). In like manner Paul explains that "though our outer man is decaying, yet our inner man is being renewed day by day" (II Cor. 4:16). Some have taken these verses as their primary documentation to posit a dichotomy of man's constitution, and to deny the three-fold designation of man's capacity for life-function. They explain that "soul" and "spirit" are but synonyms which refer to the "inner man," and cannot be differentiated. Eventually, though, they must admit that there is a difference between the psychological function of man and the spiritual function of man. Otherwise, psychological therapy is the salvation of man, and Sigmund Freud is our Savior. God forbid! Scripture is quite clear in the differentiating of these capacities of life-function. The writer to the Hebrews explains that "the Word of God (Jesus Christ) is living and active and sharper than any two-edged sword, piercing as far as the division of soul (*psuche*) and spirit (*pneuma*), of both joints and marrow, and able to judge the thoughts and intentions of the heart" (Heb. 4:12). The life-function of the soul and the life-function of the spirit are explicitly separated in this verse.

When God the Creator created man, He "formed man of dust from the ground, and breathed into his nostrils the breath of life; and man become a living soul" (Gen. 2:7). This reiterative record of man's creation is loaded with insights into man's constitution and intended function. The body of man was "formed of dust from the ground," into which God breathed the breath (or spirit) of life, and man became a behaviorly functional soul (*nephesh*). The three-fold capacity of life-function is apparent in this verse; body, spirit and soul. The Hebrew word for "breath" is *n'shahmah*. This is the same word found in Proverbs 20:27 where it is translated, "The spirit (*n'shahmah*) of man is the lamp of the Lord, searching all the innermost parts of his being." Both the Hebrew and Greek languages employ a word that can be translated both "breath" and "spirit." The Greek word for "spirit" is *pneuma*, from which we get such English words as "pneumatic" and "pneumonia," which refer to air and breathing. Additionally it can be noted that when God "breathed the spirit of life" into man, the word for "life" in the original Hebrew text is plural in number. This would seem to represent that God imparted to man His own triune life of Father, Son and Holy Spirit, so that man might function as God intended. The Greek translation of the Old Testament, the Septuagint (LXX), uses the Greek word *zoe* as the word for "life" in Genesis 2:7, along with a derivative of the same word to explain that man "became spiritually alive in his behavioral life-function of the soul."

The Greek language had several words which we translate into English as "life." These different words helped to clarify the capacity of life-function at the differing levels. The Greek word *bios* referred primarily to physical life (cf. Luke 8:14: I Tim. 2:2; II Tim. 2:4). It is the word from which we get the English words "biology," "biography," "biosphere," etc., all having to do with physical life. The Greek word *psuche* has been previously noted as referring to behavioral life-function. It is the word from which we get the English words "psyche," "psychology," etc., referring to behavioral function. The third Greek word translated into English as "life" is the word *zoe*. This is somewhat misleading since this is the word from which we derive such English words as "zoo" and "zoology" referring to animals. In the New Testament, however, it is used to refer to the spiritual life that is in Jesus Christ. "In Him was life (*zoe*), and the life (*zoe*) was the light of men" (John 1:4). "I am the way, the truth and the life (*zoe*)," Jesus said (John 14:6). "I came that you might have life (*zoe*), and have it more abundantly" (John 10:10). "These things are written that you might believe that Jesus is the Christ, the Son of God; and that believing you may have life (*zoe*) in His name" (John 20:31). "He who has the Son has the life (*zoe*); he who does not have the Son of God does not have the life (*zoe*)" (I John 5:12). By these three words the Greeks could distinguish between the three capacities of life-function in man, whereas by translating all three of them as "life" in English, we fail to thus differentiate.

Early Christian writers clearly understood these capacities of life-function within man. Tertullian, for example, who lived *circa* A.D. 150-220, explained that the body was the area of "world-consciousness," the soul was the area of "personal-consciousness," and the spirit was the area of "God-consciousness." In creating man with these three capacities of life-function, God intended that man might behave on a different basis from all other forms of His creation. Man was created with the capacity for spiritual life-function so that the very presence of the Spirit of God might dwell within the spirit of man in order to activate the character of God within the behavioral life-function of man's soul and allow such to be expressed in man's external behavior of the body unto the glory of God. As the highest order of creation, mankind was designed with the capacity to incorporate the spiritual life of God within his spirit, and express God's character of love, joy, peace, patience, etc. (cf. Gal. 5:22,23) in his behavior, as no other part of the created order is capable of doing.

The spiritual impartation of God's life into this capacity for spiritual life-function in man, in the spirit of man, was expressed by God's "breathing the breath (or spirit, *n'shahmah*) of life" into man (Gen. 2:7) at his creation. It is also expressed in the initial account of God's creation of man in the first chapter of Genesis: "Then God said, 'Let Us make man in Our image, according to Our likeness;...' And God created man in His own image, in the image of God He created him; male and female He created them" (Gen. 1:26,27). The "image of God" has been much debated in Christian theology, but the primary fallacy has been to consider man and find something about man that is like God. Suggestions of such include upright stature, spirituality, rationality, emotion, volition, personality, moral determination, sociability, masculinity, etc. Perhaps the best English translation of "image" is "visage" or "visibility." When Paul explains that "Christ is the image of God" (Col. 1:15; II Cor. 4:4), he is noting that Jesus Christ is the incarnate visible expression of the invisible character of God. When God created man and "breathed into him the spirit of lives" (Hebrew plural) (Gen. 2:7), investing him with the living spiritual presence of the Father, Son and

Holy Spirit, He did so with the intent that man might choose to allow for the visible expression of the invisible character of God within His behavior, thus allowing God to be glorified by the expression of His all-glorious character, the purpose for which we were created (Isa. 43:7). We are created with the capacity of spiritual life-function, in order to allow the spiritual character of God to be "imaged" and "visibly expressed" in our behavior.

It is important to remember that this is not an inherent capability of man to express God's character and "be like God." We are created with the capacity for spiritual life-function, and initially God invested His presence in man's spirit, but God also created us with freedom of choice to decide whether we would respond in contingency, dependency and receptivity in order to derive the divine character expression from His indwelling presence. Man is a responsible choosing creature who was designed to choose in faith to allow God to influence his thinking, affections and decisions in such a way that the man might freely choose to allow the expression of godly character in his behavior.

Once again this obviates the difference between the function of man and animal. Animals have the capacity for physical life-function and the capacity for psychological life-function, but they do not have the capacity for spiritual life-function. The behavior of the animal is not energized and activated by spirit, but is configured into remarkable patterns of instinctual behavior. Each species of animal has these pre-programmed behavioral patterns of instinct. God could have created man with such an instinctual behavior pattern to function as God intended, but such would not have allowed for a free faith/love relationship between God and man. This is why God created man with the capacity for spiritual life-function, so that man could be energized and activated by the presence of a spiritual being that indwelt his spirit, and free to choose to allow the expression of the character of that spiritual being to be expressed in his behavior. God's intent, of course, was that His own invisible, all-glorious character might be expressed visibly in the behavior of man as man freely chose to bear His "image" and glorify God. The freedom of choice, however, necessitates an alternative.

If we do not understand the constitution of man as comprised of the capacities of spiritual life-function, psychological life-function and physical life-function, in spirit and soul and body, then we will remain befuddled in understanding man's function and behavior. Ambiguities concerning man's constitution and function in both religious and psychological studies have long hindered explanations of man's behavior and the clear presentation of the gospel of Jesus Christ.

DIAGRAM

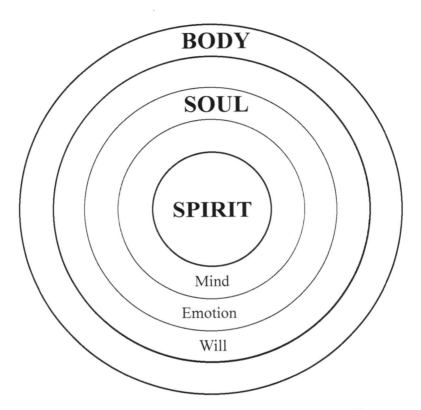

Every two-dimensional diagram is inadequate to illustrate the constitution of man and the capacities of life-function in man. This diagram of concentric circles, though inadequate, still serves a constructive purpose in providing a visible tool for conceptualization, as long as the life-functions are not conceived as "parts" or "compartments."

22

3

The Fall of Man

Created as a human being with capacity for physiological, psychological and spiritual life-function, man is the highest order of creation. Man was created so that he could express the character of God in a manner that no other creature on earth could do. Endued with the life of the Spirit of God within his capacity for spiritual life, man was intended to allow God to influence his thinking, his affections, and his decisions in order to allow the character of God to be manifested in his external behavior to the glory of God. Love, joy, peace, patience, kindness, goodness, etc. (Gal. 5:22,23) could be evidenced within interpersonal relationships as God was allowed to activate godly behavior in man.

In order for this to take place man would have to exercise the freedom of choice with which he had been created. Only God has absolute "free will" to do anything He pleases (consistent with His character), but only as a choosing creature who could freely determine to receive or not to receive God's character could man have the interpersonal relationship with God and with other men that God intended for man. Man would have to choose to be contingent and dependent upon God in order to derive God's character in his behavior. Man functions by receptivity. He is a faith-creature. He is responsible to choose from which spiritual source He will derive his spiritual condition and behavioral expression – who he is, and what he does. That choice of contingency will determine whether man will derive his activation of identity and behavior from the spiritual source of either God or Satan.

God placed the original man that He had created into a garden in Eden (Gen. 2:8). In that garden God caused trees to grow which were aesthetically pleasing to man and beneficial for physical nourishment. Two trees are specifically mentioned and labeled as the "tree of life" and the "tree of the knowledge of good and evil" (Gen. 2:9). While admitting that these labels are not the botanical designations of class or species, neither do we have to go to the opposite extreme and indicate that these trees are just "myths with a message." These two trees were likely two tangible trees in the garden, designated with particular labels in order to indicate that they represented a dichotomy of choice for mankind, a choice of behavioral expression and spiritual condition. Both trees were located in the middle of the garden (Gen. 2:9; 3:3) in order to focus man's attention upon this choice.

In providing man with this choice God was not being capricious. He was not trying to "trip man up." God was not tempting man. "Let no man say, 'I am being tempted by God,' ...for God does not tempt anyone" (James 1:13). He was giving man the opportunity to function as the choosing creature that He had created him to be, who would have to live with the consequences of his choices. In that sense, God was "testing" man, to ascertain whether man would choose to be man as God intended man to be, deriving all from God. God was giving man "the benefit of the doubt," the opportunity to doubt that he needed God in order to function as intended.

In that ideal and idyllic setting of the garden, man could never blame the frustration of the environment or the exhaus-

24

tion of his body and soul for the choice that he would make. Man could never say, "But I was so tired, I wasn't thinking straight." There was a perfect freedom in which to choose from the two alternatives.

That God presented two clear-cut alternatives for man's choice is also important. There was not just one tree of prohibition and limitation which provided a "Thou shalt not...or else!" Neither was there a singular tree which represented God's intent, and a choice of man to "Take it or leave it!" The two alternative trees indicated a genuine viable choice for man that was not just a singular, simple "Yes or No" of obedience or disobedience, but a complex choice of one or the other and the consequences thereof. God made it clear what His intent and preference for man was by encouraging man to "eat freely" (Gen. 2:16) from the tree of life, and discouraging man from eating of the tree of the knowledge of good and evil by warning him that the consequences of such a choice would alienate him from the life that he had from God. "From the tree of the knowledge of good and evil you shall not eat, for in the day that you eat from it you shall surely die" (Gen. 2:17).

The Tree of Life

The "tree of life" is often neglected in theological expositions of the choice that man faced in the garden. Such omission of consideration of the "tree of life" is more than mere neglect, for it seems to stem from theological presuppositions that have posited man's choice as a simple choice of obedience or disobedience either by repudiation of the "tree of the knowledge of good and evil" or by partaking of the fruit of that tree. Such a law and commandment-based perspective of obedience and disobedience, fails to account for the ontological factors that were involved in the choice that man was to make.

When God breathed into man "the breath of life" (Gen. 2:7), the spiritual Being of God, the triune expression of divine life, was present as the spiritual life-function of man. The divine life and Being of God was indwelling man's spirit as the potential dynamic of man's psychological and external behavior. The "tree of life" did not represent a "type" of spiritual conversion, for man already had the spiritual life of God which had been inbreathed. The word for "life" used in Genesis 2:7 in reference to the "breath of life" is identical to the word for "life" employed in Genesis 2:9 in reference to the "tree of life." The choice of man at the "tree of life" was not a choice for the initial receipt of God's life, but a choice to be ontologically receptive to the life-Being of God expressed in the soul and body function of man's behavior. The "tree of life" could not have represented a choice for regeneration or justification, as some have suggested, but had to represent a choice of deriving God's life in human behavior unto sanctification, being "set apart to function as God intended" by allowing the Holy character of God to be expressed in the behavior of man. It was the choice of "abundant life" (John 10:10) whereby man would be "saved by His life" (Rom. 5:10). The choice presented to man at the "tree of life" was the choice to allow for the divine out-working of the divinely in-breathed life of God in man.

Further explanation can be facilitated by referring to the "Life and Death" diagram on page 40.

The spiritual condition of the original man was such that the "personal resource of God's life" was present as the dynamic for spiritual life-function within the spirit of man. God had breathed into man the spirit of His life as Father, Son and Holy Spirit. The "tree of life" represented the choice

26

to allow for the behavioral expression of God's life in man's behavior, the "prevailing ramifications of God's life." The ontological dynamic of God's indwelling life could become operational in the psychological and physiological life-function of man's behavior. The "law of the spirit of life" (Rom. 8:2) would be activated in order to express the behavioral manifestations of "abundant life" (John 10:10). The free-flow of divine life functioning in man would provide no basis for corruption or mortality, for these are predicated on the absence of the life and character of God. Death is a result of the corruption of sin (Gen. 2:17; Rom. 6:23). Man's choice of the "tree of life" would have allowed for the "perpetual representation of God's eternal life" in man, and he would have "lived forever" (Gen. 3:22), expressing the immortality of God's life (I Tim. 6:16).

Partaking of the fruit of the "tree of life" would have been a choice to assimilate God's life throughout the entirety of man's functionality. Jesus was expressing similar imagery when He spoke of "eating His flesh and drinking His blood" (John 6:53), and thus participating in "eternal life" (John 6:54) in order to "live forever" (John 6:58) and "never hunger and never thirst" (John 6:35). The symbolism is of the ontological life-expression of God within the behavioral function of mankind.

Some have questioned whether the original man might have chosen to partake of the "tree of life" prior to partaking of the "tree of the knowledge of good and evil." The Scriptures do not indicate that he did so, and further speculative conjecturing of such hypothetical scenarios serve only to dissipate the importance of the choice presented to man by the two trees. In light of the "prevailing ramifications" and "perpetual representation" of God's life indicated by man's partaking of the "tree of life," such prior choosing would seem doubtful. If man had chosen to partake of the "tree of life," he would have been choosing to be receptive to and contingent upon the life of God in a freely-chosen faith/love relationship. The divine life of God in the spirit of the original man was present by creational imputation, so the choice of the "tree of life" was a choice to accept such and allow for the functional expression of God's life in the behavior of man; deity functioning within humanity as God intended.

The importance of the symbolism of the "tree of life" seems to be verified by the numerous references to this tree throughout the rest of the Scriptures. The wisdom literature refers to the "tree of life" in conjunction with "wisdom" (Prov. 3:18), the "fruit of righteousness" (Prov. 11:30), "fulfilled desires" (Prov. 13:12), and a "healing tongue" (Prov. 15:4), all of which relate to the sanctification process of God's character being expressed in man's behavior. The Revelation pictures the "tree of life" by the river in the middle of the New Jerusalem (Rev. 22:2), indicating that those who have "washed their robes" in the washing of regeneration (Titus 3:5) "have a right to the tree of life" (Rev. 22:14), partaking of and expressing the character of God's life. Such privilege can be taken away from those who reject the realities of God's life revealed in Jesus Christ (Rev. 22:19). The "tree of life" continues throughout the scriptural record as the symbol of an active and ontological partaking of God's life in order to allow God's character to be expressed in human behavior and thus to function as God intended.

Original man was encouraged to partake of the "tree of life" and had the unhindered freedom of choice to do so. The "tree of life" represented the choice to accept God's indwelling provision and the spiritual relationship and identity which that entailed, as well as the choice to depend on God's provision in a contingency of faith in order to derive

28

the expression of divine character in the behavior of man. It was a choice to allow for the divine out-working of the divinely in-breathed life of God in man.

The Tree of the Knowledge of Good and Evil

The alternative choice to that preferred and intended by God for man was the opposite ontological option. It was not merely an epistemological choice framed in a juridical context of legal obedience or disobedience based on the rejection or acceptance of this option. The choice of the "tree of the knowledge of good and evil" also had ontic implications for the spiritual condition and behavioral expression of man. The choice of the "tree of life" was the choice of obedience, to "listen under" God, depend upon God, and derive all from God. The choice of the "tree of the knowledge of good and evil" was the choice of disobedience, to "listen under" a spiritual being other than God, to depend upon and derive functionality from a spiritual source other than God. Thus the "one man's disobedience" (Rom. 5:19) had spiritual and behavioral implications whereby "the prince of the power of the air is now the spirit working in the sons of disobedience" (Eph. 2:2).

If man would not choose to be dependent upon God's life at the "tree of life," he would still be a contingent and derivative creature dependent upon a spiritual resource for his function. Man does not become independent, autonomous or self-generative. Those who suggest that man became an "independent being" by his choice of the "tree of the knowledge of good and evil" do not understand the creaturely function of humanity. They have been duped by the humanistic premise of human self-potential and self-sufficiency. Man is always a dependent and derivative creature.

29

What, then, does the "tree of the knowledge of good and evil" represent? By its label it might appear to be a rather innocuous choice, having only epistemological concern for ethical and moral content. The writer to the Hebrews encourages a maturity for Christians wherein their "senses are trained to discern good and evil" (Heb. 5:14). Why would this knowledge of "good and evil" be encouraged in Hebrews and forbidden in Genesis? This can only be understood by considering the ontological basis of good and evil. Absolute good is an attribute of the Being of God. "No one is good except God alone" (Luke 18:19). The expression of such goodness can only be derived from God's Being and the activity that expresses such. "The one who does good derives what he does out of God" (III John 11). "The fruit of the Spirit is...goodness" (Gal. 5:23). By partaking of the "tree of life" man would have known and expressed God's goodness in his behavior, deriving such from God. Man would have known "good" as that which was consistent with the character of God, and "evil" as that which was contrary to the character of God, personified in the antithetical spiritual being and character of the Evil One.

The "tree of the knowledge of good and evil" must therefore represent a knowledge of such that is outside of the ontic context of God's intent. This is evidenced by the subtle solicitation of the serpent, representing Satan, the devil (Rev. 12:9; 20:2). The "father of lies" (John 8:44) suggests to the original woman that by choosing to partake of the "tree of the knowledge of good and evil," she will "be like God, knowing good and evil" (Gen. 3:5). Was this a lie? After man sinned by choosing "the tree of the knowledge of good and evil," God said, "Behold, the man has become like one of Us, knowing good and evil" (Gen. 3:22). The question must be asked: "How does God know good and evil?" Only thereby can we ascertain how man could be "like God, knowing good and evil."

God knows good and evil not by relating such to some objective standard of goodness outside of Himself, but by recognizing that goodness is that which corresponds with His own absolute character of good. Evil is that which is not consistent with who He is, and is not the expression of His character. Because God is absolute goodness, and He is independent, autonomous and self-generating in the expression of that goodness, He can "know good and evil" in reference to Himself. Man, being contingent and derivative, cannot be "like God, knowing good and evil" by defining such in terms of his own inherent character and self-activation of such. So what the serpent suggested to the original man and woman was a lie. Actually, it was a half-truth, which is always a lie. The half-truth was that man could be deceived into thinking that he could be "like God" by determining "good and evil" in reference to his own opinions, preferences, likes and dislikes, etc. Setting himself up as his own standard and center of reference, man could determine that what he found to be right, correct, pleasurable and permissible would be called "good," and what he considered to be wrong, incorrect, unpleasant and impermissible would be called "evil." Thus began all humanly determined standards of morality and ethics, as well as the belief-systems of orthodoxy and unorthodoxy. Religion has been playing this "good and evil" game of self-determined standards of "dos" and "don'ts", right and wrong, correct and incorrect ever since. It is the relativity of good and evil whereby man seeks to relate all things to himself and make them relative to his own self-centered determinations rather than to the absolute of God's character. This is the basis of the humanistic premise that posits man as his own center of reference, whereby all revolves around his individual or collective determinations. The "father of lies" foisted upon man the lie of independency and autonomy, and sought to persuade man to align with him in his self-orientation and selfishness. Isaiah explains the diabolic selfishness of Satan, who boasted, "*I* will make myself like the Most High" (Isa. 14:14). Satan is the "I-specialist." The satanic solicitation seductively sought to entice man into a character expression of self-centered self-orientation and self-sufficiency that short-circuited God's intent to express His character of love for others through man.

The original man's act of disobedience (Rom. 5:19) and sin (Rom. 5:12,16) in choosing to partake of the "tree of the knowledge of good and evil" was a derived behavioral expression. There is always an ontological spiritual derivation for the expression of every human action. Man is not an independent self. He does not self-generate his own behavioral activity. He is not the cause of his own effects, or the energizing origin of his own activity. The behavioral activity of man always expresses the nature and character of the spiritual being who generates such activity. The deception of Satan is to deceive man into thinking that he is self-generative, and that when his behavior expresses character other than that of God's character that man is generating his own sinful and evil behavioral expression. Then, reacting with blame and shame, man will masochistically berate and beat himself trying to generate something better, and all the while the destructive intent of the Destroyer is achieved. Man is not inherently evil. He is not an individualized devil who can generate sinful and evil activity in and of himself. He does, however, have freedom of choice, and is responsible for the decisions he makes concerning the spiritual being from whence he ontologically derives his behavioral expression.

The "tree of the knowledge of good and evil" represented the choice that the original man had to ontologically derive the character expression of the Evil One who relates everything selfishly to himself. It was a choice to be receptive to the behavioral out-working of a nature and character that was contrary to the character of God. God relates all to Himself, but His absolute character of goodness, righteousness and love always flows outward in expression for the good of others. Satan's character is that of self-centeredness which relates all things to himself in order to benefit himself, and it is that character that Satan sought to activate in man's behavior, and was allowed to do so by the choice man made of the "tree of the knowledge of good and evil."

Did man really have a choice? Some would emphasize the statement of God in such a way as to imply that everything was so foreordained and predestined by God as to be inevitable. God said to man, "In the day that you eat from the tree of the knowledge of good and evil, you shall surely die" (Gen. 2:17). This is not necessarily a statement of divine necessity. Was the fall of man necessitated so that God could redeem man by a predetermined plan set down "before the foundation of the world" (Eph. 1:4; Rev. 13:8)? Does God's statement imply pre-purposing or foreknowledge? The statement may indicate nothing more than a warning of the spiritual consequences that would occur within man if he exercised his freedom of choice to partake of the "tree of the knowledge of good and evil." As such it would be a simply "If...then" statement: "If you eat, then you shall die."

What did God mean by this threatened death? The Satanic serpent contradicted God's statement, saying, "You surely shall not die" (Gen. 3:4). To what extent could Adam have known what death involved? He knew what life was, for he was a participant in physiological, psychological and spiri-

33

tual life-function. Death would be the deprivation and absence of a particular life-function. Perhaps he had witnessed death as the animals ate the plants and killed other animals for food, and perhaps he had done so also. The concept of spiritual death, however, could only be perceived by Adam as the deprivation of the life that he had received by the inbreathing of God's Spirit (Gen. 2:7).

Did Adam die as God had warned, when he chose to partake of the "tree of the knowledge of good and evil"? At first it may have appeared that the serpent was correct when he said, "You surely shall not die" (Gen. 3:4). Adam was still physically alive, and lived for many years afterwards tilling the ground and fathering children. He was also quite psychologically active, thinking, feeling, and making decisions that allowed for derived behavioral expression in the activities of his body. The spiritual death that occurred within Adam when he ate of the "tree of the knowledge of good and evil" may have been almost imperceptible. "The natural man cannot understand spiritual things" (I Cor. 2:14). God was correct; Satan was the liar. In the day that man ate of the "tree of the knowledge of good and evil," he died spiritually.

What is the prerequisite for spiritual death? What is necessary for a man to die spiritually? A man cannot die on a particular life-function level if he is not previously alive on that life-function level. The prerequisite for death is pre-existent life. One cannot die spiritually if there was no spiritual life, which serves to verify that the "breath of life" breathed into man by God (Gen. 2:7) was indeed the spiritual life of God the Father, Son and Holy Spirit. When man died spiritually as God had warned would be the consequence of choosing to partake of the "tree of the knowledge of good and evil," he experienced the deprivation and absence of the spiritual life of God in the spirit of the man.

Can God's life die? No. God is eternal life. The life of God did not cease to exist; rather it was simply withdrawn from indwelling presence in the spirit of man. God moved out! He would not remain as an unwanted resident in man, though He remained the sovereign, living God of the universe.

Human misconceptions of death often paint a distorted perception of spiritual death. If death is defined as termination, annihilation or cessation of function, then the spiritual death of man implies either that the life of God was obliterated and God ceased to be, or man ceased to be man with all three levels of physiological, psychological and spiritual function. Neither is true. God was still God, and man was still man. If spiritual death is defined only on the basis of relationality with God, and explained as separation, estrangement or alienation from God, then it might appear that man is capable of functioning independently of any spiritual relationship. Impossible, for man is a dependent, contingent and derivative creature. Spiritual death is the absence of the presence of the spiritual life of God in the spirit of the man. The ontological indwelling and spiritual union of God with man is severed. But this does not leave man as a "hollow man" with a "spiritual vacuum" waiting in "dormancy." Man's spirit is not a "throneroom without a king," the "unoccupied territory" of a "container without contents," as some have referred to the spiritual condition of fallen man. Man cannot exist and function independently, so in spiritual death there was the severance of ontological dependency on God and transference to ontological dependence upon Satan for the derivation of spiritual condition and identity. It might be said that a *coup d'etat* took place in the spirit of man: God moved out and Satan moved in. The "prince of the power of the air" was now the "spirit" who was "energizing in the sons of disobedi-

35

ence" (Eph. 2:2). Spiritual death is not spiritual non-function, but is rather the absence of the spiritual function of the life of God in the spirit of man and the spiritual function of the satanic spirit in man's spirit.

(Refer again to the "Life and Death" diagram on page 40 which contrasts the implications and consequences of the "tree of life" and the "tree of the knowledge of good and evil.")

When the original man chose against partaking of the "tree of life," he chose to reject the "personal resource" of God's life in the spirit of the man. When he chose to partake of the "tree of the knowledge of good and evil," he chose to receive another "personal resource" of spiritual indwelling and identity. Man's spiritual function was now dependent upon "the one having the power of death, that is the devil" (Heb. 2:14). Paul explains that "death reigns" (Rom. 5:17) in fallen mankind. This is not a static spiritual non-function, but the "personal resource" of the "spirit of the prince of the air energizing in the sons of disobedience" (Eph. 2:2). Man was spiritually dead in his "trespasses and sins" (Eph. 2:1; Col. 2:13) and "transgressions" (Eph. 2:5), but such spiritual death is quite functional and active in its ontological identity with and energizing of the spirit of Satan.

The "personal resource of death" expresses his diabolic character and nature in the "prevailing ramifications of death" through the behavior of the soul and body of man. The "power of sin" manifests himself in the behavioral "presence of sin" as character contrary to the character of God becomes derivatively operative and is enacted in man's behavior. The "law of sin and of death" (Rom. 7:24; 8:2) is operative. "The one committing sin derives what he does from the devil" (I John 3:8). The behavioral manifestations are devoid of the life and character of God. They are "dead works" (Heb. 6:1) which "bear fruit for death" (Rom. 7:5) and "bring forth death" (James 1:15). The accumulated "dead works" of sinful expression become the collective death manifestations of the "world-system," governed by the "god of this world" (II Cor. 4:4).

As the "personal resource of death" functions in man's spirit and soul, the corruptibility of death take effect in his body, leading to physical death. When God warned man of the consequence of eating of the "tree of the knowledge of good and evil," He said, "In the day that you eat from it you shall surely die" (Gen. 2:17). More literally the Hebrew text might be translated, "In the day that you eat from it, dying you shall die," for there is a repetition of the Hebrew word for "death." Apparently God intended to indicate that spiritual death would lead to other forms of death in the life-function levels of soul and body. Degeneration sets into man's behavior and begins to affect his physiological function also. Paul explained that "the outer man is decaying" (II Cor. 4:16). Some have identified this as consistent with the "second law of thermodynamics" in science which attempts to explain the degeneration and entropy within the universe. Having died spiritually, the original man later died physically (Gen. 5:5), and those death consequences have extended to all the human race. "It is appointed for men to die once and after this comes judgment" (Heb. 9:27).

When the "power of sin" has effected the "presence of sin" within an individual, and that person dies physically while in a condition of spiritual death, then the "permanence of sin" is settled in the "perpetual representation of death," apart from the eternal presence of the life of God. This is a perpetual ontological identification with the devil and his destiny in that "eternal fire prepared for the devil and his angels"

(Matt. 25:41), the "eternal punishment" (Matt. 25:46) of "darkness forever" (Jude 1:13) in everlasting death.

After man made the choice to partake of the "tree of the knowledge of good and evil," and God confronted him with the consequences of so doing (Gen. 3:16-19), God hustled him out of the garden, "lest he stretch out his hand, and take also from the tree of life, and eat, and live forever" (Gen. 3:22). God "drove the man out; and stationed the cherubim, and the flaming sword which turned every direction, to guard the way to the tree of life" (Gen. 3:24). Why was it so important to keep man from partaking of the "tree of life" after he had partaken of the "tree of the knowledge of good and evil"? Apparently some of the factors of the "tree of life" such as "incorruptibility" and "perpetual representation" would have combined to render man a perpetual sinner who would "live forever" in his fallen condition without any possibility of redemption and restoration of God's life. God graciously and mercifully removed man from such a possibility, knowing already what He intended to do to restore His life to man by His Son, Jesus Christ.

Whereas the "tree of life" is referred to numerous times throughout the Scripture, the "tree of the knowledge of good and evil" is never mentioned again in Scripture outside of the second and third chapters of Genesis. Why is that? Once that choice was made by the original man, and the effects thereof permeated the entire human race, the choice of that tree was never necessary again. Mankind had fallen and would remain in the consequences of death until they individually received the life of God that would be made available again to man in Jesus Christ.

The restoration of God's life to man by the indwelling of the Spirit of Christ in the spirit of a man who has received Him by faith, allows for the continued choice represented by the "tree of life." The Christian continues to make the choice to be receptive to the behavioral outworking of the character of the spiritual life received in Jesus Christ.

LIFE AND DEATH

Personal Resource of Life
Spiritual life. "Breath of life" (Gen. 2:7)
The Life of God in the spirit of man.

Prevailing Ramifications of Life
1. Principle of life.
   Life is made operational in behavior. cf. Rom. 8:2

2. Expression of life.
   Behavioral manifestations.
   "Abundant life" – John 10:10

3. Incorruptibility of life.
   "Live forever" (Gen. 3:22)
   No death.

Perpetual Representation of Life.
Eternal life.

SPIRIT

SOUL

BODY

Personal Resource of Death
Spiritual death. "The one having the power of death, that is the devil" (Heb. 2:14) cf. Eph. 2:2

Prevailing Ramifications of Death
1. Principle of death.
   Death is made operational in behavior. "Law of sin and of death" (Rom. 7:24; 8:2)

2. Expression of death
   Behavioral manifestations.
   "Dead works" (Heb. 6:1)
   "Fruit for death" (Rom. 7:5)
   "brings forth death" (James 1:15).

3. Corruptibility of death
   "Dying, you shall die" (Gen. 2:17)
   "Adam died" (Gen. 5:5)
   "appointed to die" (Heb. 9:27)

Perpetual Representation of Death
Everlasting death.
"Eternal punishment" (Matt. 25:46)
"darkness forever" (Jude 1:13).

4

The Natural Man

How did the choice that Adam made in the garden affect the entire human race? Adam rejected the option represented by the "tree of life," to allow for the out-working of the divinely in-breathed life of God in his behavior. Instead, he chose the "tree of the knowledge of good and evil," representing a choice to derive his spiritual condition and behavioral expression from a spiritual source other than God. Acting as the original man, he represented the entire human race in the choice that he made. The consequences of sin and death that were activated in Adam were not limited to him individually, but were collectively applied to all of mankind.

Adamic Solidarity of the Natural Man

That our physical ancestry is to be traced back to the original man who was the genetic "father of the human race" and the "seminal head" of mankind, is not difficult to understand. But in what sense is the natural spiritual condition of humanity attributable to, and a consequence of, Adam's choice of sin? The spiritual solidarity of mankind with the fallen spiritual condition of the original man is a more difficult concept for many contemporary men to grasp.

The Hebrews often thought in terms of the actions of a previous ancestor affecting future generations of descendants. Making the argument for the supremacy of the Melchizedekian priesthood over the Levitical priesthood, the writer of the epistle to the Hebrews argues that Levi, while "still in the loins of his father (great-grandfather), Abraham, paid tithes to Melchizedek" (Heb. 7:9,10). Levi was regarded to be "in Abraham," and therefore the actions of Abraham were regarded as inclusive of all his descendancy. Where was Levi when Abraham paid tribute to the priesthood of Melchizedek? He was "in Abraham." When Abraham was blessed by Melchizedek, Levi was blessed by Melchizedek. So where were you and I when Adam sinned? We were "in Adam." When Adam sinned and incurred the consequences of death, we sinned "in Adam," and incurred the consequences of spiritual death.

Some varieties of Arminian theology assert that every individual man is born spiritually innocent with the potential of being either sinful or good. They allege that if man were to make the right choices from the time of his birth, he could live a perfect life. This is an example of the humanistic premise of man's self-potentiality, whereby every individual person is independent, autonomous and self-generative of his condition and behavior. They fail to recognize that man is dependent and contingent, always deriving his spiritual condition and behavioral expression from a spiritual source.

The scriptures affirm that mankind is born physically in spiritual solidarity with the original man, Adam. The consequences of death, beginning with the "personal resource" of spiritual death, are imputed to all men because Adam was the "Representative Head" or "Federal Head" of the human race. The source of this spiritual death is "the one having the power of death, that is the devil" (Heb. 2:14), and as such "death reigns" (Rom. 5:17,21) throughout the life-function levels of mankind in their natural state.

Jude explains that those who are "natural" are "devoid of the Spirit" of God (Jude 1:19). But man cannot live in a spiritual void or vacuum; he is always spiritually derivative and contingent. In the absence of God's Spirit, the opposing spirit of Satan becomes operative in the spiritual life-function of the natural man. Thus it is that James refers to a "natural" wisdom that "does not come down from above," from God, but is "demonic" (James 3:15). The natural man functions on the basis of diabolic energizing. Paul explains that "the natural man does not accept the things of the Spirit of God; for they are foolishness to him, and he cannot understand them, because they are spiritually appraised" (I Cor. 2:14). Only when the Spirit of Christ indwells and is operative in the Christian can he understand and accept God's wisdom, for then "Christ becomes to us wisdom from God" (I Cor. 1:24,30). Christians "have received, not the spirit of the world (of the "god of this world" - II Cor. 4:4), but the Spirit who is from God, that we might know the things freely given to us by God" (I Cor. 2:12).

The original man, you will recall, was created to bear the image of God, in order to glorify God by allowing the character of God to be expressed through the behavior of the man. "God created man in His own image, in the image of God He created him" (Gen. 1:26,27). In order to visibly express the character of an invisible God in the behavior of man, the presence of the Spirit of God would have to dwell in the spirit of man in order to generate His character. God alone is the source of His own character! Godliness must be derived from God! After Adam sinned by eating of the "tree of the knowledge of good and evil," all of his descendants were natural men who were "devoid of the Spirit" (Jude

43

1:19), "excluded from the life of God" (Eph. 4:18). As such they could not bear the visible expression of the character of God. In the absence of the Spirit of God, they are indwelt by the evil spirit whose image of character they express in their behavior.

Adam's first two descendants were Cain and Abel (Gen. 4:1,2). The visible expression of character exhibited by Cain was not derived from God in order to image God. Sin was operative in Cain, creating an anger and jealousy that prompted Cain to kill his brother, Abel (Gen. 4:5-8). Such was not the expression of the character of God, but the character of the spirit of evil. "Cain derived what he did out of the Evil One, and slew his brother" (I John 3:12). Cain was not visibly expressing and imaging the character of God, but instead was visibly expressing and imaging the character of Satan, who "was a murderer from the beginning" (John 8:44). When Adam and Eve had another son "in place of Abel" (Gen. 4:25), Adam "became the father of a son in his own likeness, according to his image, and named him Seth" (Gen. 5:3). Adam's sons did not come into being with the presence of the Spirit of God in their spirit in order to image the character of God, but like their spiritually fallen father they came into being with the presence of the evil spirit of Satan as the "personal resource of death" within them, and they consequently expressed and imaged the likeness of the character of the Evil One.

When Paul explains the spiritual condition and behavioral expression of the Ephesians prior to their becoming Christians, he writes, "And you were dead (spiritually) in your trespasses and sins, in which you formerly walked according to the course of this world (of which Satan is "god" - II Cor. 4:4), according to the prince of the power of the air (Satan), of the spirit (the "spirit of this world" - I Cor. 2:12) that is now working in the sons of disobedience (all mankind due to Adam's disobedience - Rom. 5:19). Among them we too all formerly lived in the lusts of our flesh, indulging the desires of the flesh and of the mind, and were by nature (the spiritual nature of the Evil One) children of wrath, even as the rest" (Eph. 2:1-3). The natural, unregenerate man functions by spiritual derivation from the spirit of Satan.

The most comprehensive passage of Scripture that explains the condition of all mankind predicated on the choice of sin that Adam made, is to be found in Romans 5:12-21. Paul writes that "through one man (Adam) sin entered into the world (of mankind), and death (all of the death consequences) through (Adam's) sin, and so death (all of the death consequences) spread to all men, because all (men) sinned (in Adam)" (Rom. 5:12). This is in accord with Paul's statement that "in Adam all die" (I Cor. 15:22). To the Romans, Paul continues to reiterate that "by the transgression of the one (Adam) the many (all mankind) died (all of the death consequences)" (Rom. 5:15). "The one (Adam) sinned," and "the judgment (of God) arose from one (transgression of Adam) resulting in condemnation (to all men)" (Rom. 5:16). "By the transgression of the one (Adam), death (all of the death consequences) reigned (in all mankind) through the one (Adam)" (Rom. 5:17). "Through one transgression (Adam's) there resulted condemnation to all men" (Rom. 5:18). "Through the one man's (Adam's) disobedience (at the "tree of the knowledge of good and evil") the many (all mankind) were made sinners (spiritual identity)" (Rom. 5:19). "Sin (personified resource thereof) reigned in death (all of the death consequences)" (Rom. 5:21).

It is important to note that the spiritual condition of all the natural descendants of Adam who have not been regenerated spiritually in Jesus Christ, is that of spiritual death (Rom.

5:12,14,15,17,21). The spiritual authority that is personified as the energizing source of such death is represented as "death reigning" (Rom. 5:14,17) and "sin reigning" (Rom. 5:21). The spiritual identity of the natural man when such a spiritual authority is establishing his spiritual condition, is expressed by his being "made a sinner" (Rom. 5:19). This designation does not refer to behavioral expressions of sinfulness, even though all men will inevitably express such behavioral sins because of their spiritual identity as "sinners" wherein the personification of sin and death reigns. We do not become sinners because we sin, but we sin because we are sinners!

The method by which these spiritual realities are transferred and transmitted to the entire human race from Adam has been a topic of much speculation. Perhaps the predominant explanation is based on the fact that when Jesus Christ became a man, He did not have human paternity from Joseph, and did not partake of the fallen spiritual condition of the rest of mankind. From the conjunction of these known phenomena in the life of Jesus, it is conjectured that the sinful spiritual condition of mankind is passed on by seminal transmission through the paternal seed. Can spiritual realities be conveyed genetically? Popular psychology today assumes that behavioral patterns and other psychological factors, such as homosexuality, alcoholism, etc., can be transmitted genetically. Is it not basically the same argument to indicate that spiritual realities are carried in paternal genes? God has not seen fit to inform us of the methodology of the transmission of the fallen spiritual condition of all mankind from Adam onward. Perhaps our finite understanding must rest content with the recognition of spiritual solidarity with Adam's sin and his subsequent spiritual condition, which when absent and devoid of the Spirit of God will be filled with the opposite spirit, for man is never an independent, autonomous and self-generative being.

Satanic Function in the Natural Man

The function of the satanic spirit within the spiritual condition of the fallen, natural man is often questioned. First of all, we have noted that such an understanding is logically necessitated to avoid the humanistic premise of man's independency, autonomy and self-generation (as noted in the first chapter). Man was created by the Creator God to be spiritually and behaviorally dependent, contingent and derivative. When, by the sin of Adam, all men became spiritually dead, without the presence of the Spirit of God, mankind did not become independent and able to generate his own behavioral character. Man did not assume the function of God, or become a god. Neither did man become sub-human, or become an animal without any spiritual function, for he does not have the required instinctual pattern to thus behave as an animal. Those who describe man's spiritual condition apart from God as a spiritual vacuum or void, relegate fallen man to a non-human entity. Fallen man remains functional spiritually, psychologically and physiologically. Christian teaching has long been ambiguous about how mankind functions apart from God. Sometimes the theologians have admitted some manner of outside satanic influence upon the unregenerate, but have denied an indwelling satanic presence in the spirit of non-Christians. Another explanation is to turn the sin-problem into a self-problem. If man's problem is himself, then he must masochistically suppress or crucify this alleged "self" by some human performance "works" process, in order to be what God wants him to be. This is but an adapted form of "evangelical humanism" that posits that man is self-generative of his own sin. These are inadequate and unbiblical explanations.

There seems to be abundant biblical documentation that points to the spiritual activity of Satan within the natural man. When we recognize this, we can understand that man remains a dependent, contingent and derivative creature even in his unregenerate state of spiritual function. The following biblical documentation will be formatted in contrasts and comparisons between the spiritual condition of the regenerate and unregenerate, between Christians and non-Christians.

Spiritual union - The Christian is identified as being "in Christ," using the Greek preposition *en.* Jesus refers to our "abiding in (*en*) the vine" (John 15:4), and Paul explains that "if any man be in (*en*) Christ, he is a new creature (II Cor. 5:17). In contrast, John notes that "the whole world lies in (*en*) the Evil One" (I John 5:19).

Spiritual indwelling - Again using the Greek preposition *en*, Paul writes that the mystery of the gospel for the Christian is "Christ in (*en*) you, the hope of glory" (Col. 1:27), and asks, "Do you not recognize that Jesus Christ is in (*en*) you?" (II Cor. 13:5). The spiritual indwelling of Satan in the unregenerate seems to be evident from the contrasting statement of "the prince of the power of the air, the spirit now working in (*en*) the sons of disobedience" (Eph. 2:2).

Spiritual source - The Greek preposition *ek* refers to source, origin or derivation. Paul indicates that we are "not adequate in ourselves to consider anything as coming from (*ek* - out of) ourselves, but our adequacy is from (*ek* - out of) God" (II Cor. 3:5). On the other hand, John writes that "the one who practices sin is of (*ek* - out of) the devil" (I John

3:8), and "Cain was of (*ek* - out of) the Evil One, and slew his brother" (I John 3:12).

Spiritual nature - Though we often hear references to "human nature," it is more biblical to recognize that the spiritual nature of man is the nature of the spirit who indwells him. Using the Greek word *phusis,* Peter affirms that Christians are "partakers of the divine nature (*phusis*)" (II Peter 1:4). Prior to becoming Christians, Paul explained that we "were by nature (*phusis*) children of wrath" (Eph. 2:3).

Spiritual treasure - Most will be familiar with the word "thesaurus" which refers to a treasury of synonyms and antonyms. The Greek word *thesaurus* is used when Paul affirms that Christians "have this treasure (*thesaurus*) in earthen vessels" (II Cor. 4:7), referring to the indwelling presence of the Spirit of Christ. Jesus explained that "the good man out of his good treasure (*thesaurus*) brings forth what is good; and the evil man out of his evil treasure (*thesaurus*) brings forth what is evil" (Matt. 12:35).

Spiritual authority - The authority for the Christian is in the Lord Jesus Christ. Jesus said, "All authority (*exousia*) has been given to Me in heaven and on earth" (Matt. 28:18). It was the risen Lord Jesus who spoke to Saul on the road to Damascus, commissioning him to convert the Gentiles "that they may turn from darkness to light and from the dominion (*exousia*) of Satan to God" (Acts 26:18). Conversion is the turning from the spiritual authority of Satan to the spiritual authority of God in Christ.

Spiritual energizing - The English words "energy" and "energize" are derived from the Greek word *energeo.* Writing to the Philippian Christians, Paul says, "God is at work (*ener-geo* - energizing) in you, both to will and to work (*energeo*) for His good pleasure" (Phil. 2:13). Reminding the Ephesians of their previous spiritual condition, Paul refers to "the spirit now working (*energeo* - energizing) in the sons of disobedience" (Eph. 2:2).

Spiritual relationship - The Christian can cry "Abba, Father (*pater*)" (Rom. 8:15), but Jesus told the unregenerate religionists, "You are of your father (*pater*), the devil" (John 8:44). "The Spirit Himself bears witness with our spirit that we (Christians) are children (*tekna*) of God" (Rom. 8:16), whereas those who are not "children (*tekna*) of God" are "children (*tekna*) of the devil" (I John 3:10).

Spiritual personage - It is the personal experience of the Christian that "the Spirit (*pneuma*) bears witness with our spirit that we are children of God" (Rom. 8:16). "We have not received the spirit (*pneuma*) of the world, but the Spirit (*pneuma*) who is from God" (I Cor. 2:12). Those who do not know Jesus Christ have "the spirit (*pneuma*) that works in the sons of disobedience" (Eph. 2:2).

Spiritual power - For Christians, "Christ is the power (*dunamis*) of God" (I Cor. 1:24), as contrasted with the "powers (*dunamis*)" that contradict our derived power. By Christ's indwelling we have "the surpassing greatness of His power (*kratos*)" (Eph. 1:19), but the one having "the power (*kratos*) of death is the devil" (Heb. 2:14).

Spiritual wisdom - Christ has become our spiritual wisdom (*sophia*) in the Christian life (I Cor. 1:30). There are others, though, whose wisdom (*sophia*) is "natural and demonic" (James 3:15).

Spiritual will - The spiritual personage within us has a particular spiritual objective or will that he seeks to activate within our behavior. For Christians, "God is at work in you, both to will (*thelo*) and to work for His good pleasure" (Phil. 2:13). In opposition to such are those for whom Paul prays that "God might grant them repentance leading to the knowledge of the truth, and they may come to their senses and escape from the snare of the devil, having been held captive by him to do his will (*thelema*)" (II Tim. 2:25,26).

Spiritual works - Paul explains that Christians have been "created in Christ Jesus for good works (*ergon*), which God prepared beforehand, that we should walk in them" (Eph. 2:10). Jesus exposed the Jewish religious leaders by exclaiming, "You are doing the deeds (*ergon*) of your father, the devil" (John 8:41,44).

In addition to these comparative references which utilize the same Greek word to draw the contrast between the spiritual condition of the regenerate and unregenerate, there are numerous other references which utilize opposite words to reveal the contrast of spiritual condition. A few examples will suffice.

Darkness/light - Satan is identified with the realm of darkness. This is evident in the text already cited where the risen Lord Jesus tells Saul that he will turn Gentiles "from darkness to light, from the dominion of Satan to God" (Acts 26:18). Christians have been "delivered from the domain of darkness, and transferred to the kingdom of His beloved Son"

51

(Col. 1:13). We were "formerly darkness, but are now children of light" (Eph. 5:8).

Death/life - It has previously been explained that "the one having the power of death is the devil" (Heb. 2:14), so the condition of spiritual death is not cessation of function, but the activity of Satan. On the other hand, Jesus declares, "I am...the life" (John 14:6). When the Spirit of Christ indwells the Christian, "Christ is our life" (Col. 3:4). "We have passed out of death into life" (I John 3:14).

Sin/righteousness - The spiritual identity of the natural man has been noted in his being "made a sinner" (Rom. 5:19). The personified presence of sin is operative spiritually in the unregenerate, for "sin reigns" (Rom. 5:21) in those who are "slaves of sin" (Rom. 6:17), and who "commit sin, deriving what they do from the devil" (I John 3:8). Christians, on the other hand, have been "freed from sin" (Rom. 6:18) and "made righteous" (II Cor. 5:21) by the indwelling presence of the "Righteous One" (I John 2:1).

Lie/truth - Satan is "a liar, and the father of lies" (John 8:44). Unregenerate men have "exchanged the truth of God for the lie" (Rom. 1:25). The "spirit of error" (I John 4:6) is at work in the natural man. A Christian has been regenerated by the reception of the "spirit of truth" (John 14:17; I John 4:6), the indwelling presence of Jesus Christ who said, "I am...the truth" (John 14:6), who continues to "guide us into all the truth" (John 16:13).

The foregoing comparisons and contrasts are not an exhaustive listing of the biblical evidence that supports the satanic activity within the unregenerate in like manner as the

52

Spirit of God functions within the Christian. The reader may wish to search the Scriptures for additional documentation of these spiritual realities.

Despite the Biblical evidence many Christian teachers continue to deny the satanic function within the natural man. They refer instead to an ambiguous "principle" of death, sin or evil that is supposedly operative in the person apart from Jesus Christ. Often they propose that the origin of sinfulness is in the "straw-man" which they call "self." The logical response to these unbiblical suggestions is to ask, "If man can generate or originate his own sin or evil-character, then why is he not equally able to generate or originate righteous character?" The one, like the other, is independently and autonomously self-generated character. If man can self-generate sin and evil, he is the devil. If he can self-generate righteousness, he is God, and has no need for Jesus Christ, the Righteous. Man is not devil and man is not God; he is a dependent and derivative creature who is always contingent on spiritual presence to function by receptivity, and to thereby manifest the character of the spiritual personage on whom he is reliant.

If there is sin apart from the personal sin-source of Satan, if there is evil apart from the Evil One, if there is death apart from the one having the power of death, that is the devil, if there is lying apart from the one who is the father of lies; then there must be life apart from the One who is Life, there must be truth apart from the One who is Truth, there must be righteousness apart from the Righteous One, and there must be salvation apart from the One who is Savior. We would have to draw the same outlandish conclusion that Paul proposed, based on his opponent's arguments, that "Christ died needlessly" (Gal. 2:21). This evidences how important the understanding of the theodicy of the satanic function in the natural man really is, in order to maintain an accurate grasp of the gospel.

Most of those who react to and reject the satanic function within unbelievers mistakenly think that such diminishes the responsibility of man. Such is not the case. Differentiation must be made between the spiritual-generation of a man's spiritual condition and behavioral expression, and the volitional determination whereby man is responsible to choose and decide his course of action, i.e. from whence he will derive his condition and activity by receptivity, with freedom of choice. To accept the biblical statements of spiritual condition and behavioral activity as derived from either God or Satan is not to deny the responsibility of man to exercise freedom of choice. Theologians distinguish between the *prima causa* of Satan's energizing of sin and the *causa secunda* of human responsibility for sin.

Having briefly reiterated the logical necessity of the satanic function within the natural man, and set forth some of the biblical documentation for such, it will now be instructive to note some of the theological affirmations of this same reality. By the following quotations it can be documented that this has been taught in Christian theology throughout the history of the church:

Blaise Pascal - *Provincial Letters.*

"Whom do you wish to be taken for? – for children of the gospel, or for the enemies of the gospel? You must be ranged either on the one side or on the other; for there is no medium here. 'He that is not with Jesus Christ is against Him.' Into these two classes all mankind are divided. There are, according to St. Augustine, two peoples and two worlds. There is the world of the children of God, who form one body, of which Jesus Christ is the king and the head; and there is the world at enmity with God, of which the devil is

54

the king and the head. Hence Jesus Christ is called the King and God of the world, because he has everywhere his subjects and worshippers; and hence the devil is also termed in Scripture the prince of this world, and the god of this world, because he has everywhere his agents and his slaves.

...those who are on the side of Jesus Christ have, as St. Paul teaches us, the same mind which was also in him; and those who are the children of the devil, who has been a murderer from the beginning, according to the saying of Jesus Christ, follow the maxims of the devil."[1]

John Calvin - *Commentary on Genesis.*

"The Scripture everywhere calls them 'dead,' who, being oppressed by the tyranny of sin and Satan, breath nothing but their own destruction."[2]

John Calvin - *Institutes of the Christian Religion.*

"The devil is said to have undisputed possession of this world. ..he is said to blind all those who do not believe the gospel, and to do his own work in the children of disobedience. ..all the wicked are vessels of wrath...they are said to be of their father, the devil. For as believers are recognized to be the sons of God by bearing His image, so the wicked are properly regarded as the children of Satan, from having degenerated into his image."[3]

John Calvin - *The Gospel According to John.*

"As we are called the children of God, not only because we resemble Him, but because He governs us by His Spirit, because Christ lives and is vigorous in us, so as to conform us to His Father's image; so, on the other hand, the devil is said to be the father of those whose understandings he blinds, whose hearts he moves to commit all unrighteousness, and on whom, in short, he acts powerfully and exercises his tyranny."[4]

Emanuel V. Gerhart - *Institutes of the Christian Religion.*

"Those who choose to ascribe such appalling inhumanity and diabolism exclusively to Jews and Gentiles, (instead of referring it to a mighty personal evil spirit, as its background,) do not get rid, as they suppose, of a devil. Then man is himself resolved into a devil; for he is invested with a kind and degree of malice which dehumanizes human nature, turns earth into pandemonium, and history into an interminable war of incarnated fiends."[5]

Francis Pieper - *Christian Dogmatics.*

"The entire state of unbelief – among heathen nations as well as in external Christendom – is a work of the devil (Eph. 2:1,2). All who do not believe the Gospel are thinking and doing what the devil wills; they are completely in his power (Acts 26:18; Col. 1:13). And the fact that men do not know this, yes, even deny the existence of the devil, is likewise due to the operation of the devil. ...we must never forget that every unbeliever is completely in the power of Satan, until God's grace and power delivers him from the power of Satan and translates him into the kingdom of His dear Son (Col. 1:13).[6]

"According to Scripture the cause of sin in man is the devil. He sinned first and then seduced man. And he is still the power impelling unbelievers to sin and tempting believers to sin. Christ tells the unbelieving Jews, (John 8:44) "Ye are of your father the devil." Because he seduced men to sin, the devil is called a "murderer from the beginning" (John 8:44); and since he is the *prima causa peccati,* the inventor of sin, we call sin, with good reason, a 'work of the devil,' even in the case of sins committed by believers. That such is the case is clearly indicated by Christ when He says to Peter, who sought to keep Christ from suffering and dying: "Get thee behind Me, Satan" (Matt. 16:23).[7]

"All unbelievers are dead in sins, and Satan is the ruling power in them (Eph. 2:1-3; Col. 1:13; Acts 26:18)."[8]

William Cooke - *Christian Theology.*

"Satan means adversary. He is called "Apollyon," which means Destroyer, because he delighteth in destroying the souls of men, and "goeth about as a roaring lion, seeking whom he may devour." All the sin and misery of our world..., and all the sin and misery of its future history, and all the misery of hell, is not only the result of his agency and influence, but results in that which he and his minion find their gratification."[9]

E.H. Bancroft - *Elemental Theology.*

"Unredeemed men are in helpless captivity to sin and Satan and are regarded as children of the devil."[10]

Augustus H. Strong - *Systematic Theology.*

"Self-originated sin would have made man himself a Satan."[11]

A.W. Pink - *Gleanings in Genesis.*

"Man is not an independent creature, for he did not make himself."[12]

A.W. Pink - *Gleanings From the Scriptures.*

"...death brought its subjects under complete bondage to sin and Satan... They were not guided by the Holy Spirit, but energized and directed by the evil spirit..."[13]

"It (the Bible) reveals that men are morally the devil's children (Acts 13:10; I John 3:10), that they are his captives

(II Tim. 2:26) and under his power (Acts 26:18; Col. 1:13), that they are determined to do what he wants (John 8:44). He is described as the strong man armed, who holds undisputed possession of the sinner's soul, until a stronger than he dispossesses him (Luke 11:21-22). It speaks of men being 'oppressed of the devil' (Acts 10:38), and declares, 'The god of this world hath blinded the minds of them which believe not, lest the light of the glorious gospel of Christ, who is the image of God, should shine unto them' (II Cor. 4:4). The heart of fallen man is the throne on which Satan reigns, and the sons of Adam are naturally inclined to yield themselves slave to him."

"Since the fall this malignant spirit has entered into human nature in a manner somewhat analogous to that in which the Holy Spirit dwells in the hearts of believers. He has intimate access to our faculties... Satan can also affect from within. He is able not only to take thoughts out of men's minds (Luke 8:12), but to place thoughts in them, as we are told he 'put into the heart of Judas' to betray Christ (John 13:2); he works indiscernibly as a spirit."[14]

Louis Sperry Chafer - *Systematic Theology.*

"The unregenerate masses of humanity are said to be deceived by Satan. They are imposed upon by Satan's subterfuge, treachery, and fraud."[15]

"Little did Adam and Eve realize that, so far from attaining independence, they were becoming bondslaves to sin and Satan. From that time forth Satan was to energize them and their children to do his will (Eph. 2:1,2; Col. 1:13; I John 5:19).[16]

"Little indeed are the unregenerate prepared to recognize their present relation to Satan. Satan is described as the one who deceiveth the whole world (Rev. 12:9; 20:3,8; cf. Col. 1:13; Eph. 2:1,2). The classification, 'the children of disobedience,' refers to Adam's federal disobedience and

58

includes all of the unregenerate as disobedient and energized by Satan (II Cor. 4:3,4; I John 5:19).

"Unregenerate man is under the influence of Satan who is in authority over them, who energizes them, who blinds them concerning the gospel, and who deceives them concerning their true relation to himself."[17]

Louis Sperry Chafer - *Satan: His Motives and Methods.*

"It then may be concluded from the testimony of the Scriptures that Satan imparts his wisdom and strength to the unbelieving in the same manner as the power of God is imparted to the believer by the Holy Spirit. ...This impartation of energizing power from Satan is not toward a limited few who might be said, because of some strange conduct, to be possessed of a demon; but is the common condition of all who are yet unsaved, and are therefore still in the 'power of darkness'." ...the great mass of unsaved humanity are in the arms of Satan, and by his subtlety they are all unconscious of their position and relation."[18]

Daniel P. Fuller - *International Standard Bible Encyclopedia.*

"Satan rules in the hearts of all those who are not 'born of God' (I John 3:8f); they are called the 'children of the devil' (v. 10; cf. John 8:44). Prior to regeneration all were energized and motivated by the spirit of Satan (Eph. 2:2; cf. Acts 26:18). For the time being God has granted Satan a limited power over death, and Satan uses the fear of death to keep people in bondage to him (Heb. 2:14f.)."[19]

L. Nelson Bell, "Christianity Today" magazine.

"There are two forces contending for our minds, wills and bodies. It is a solemn thought, and one we hate to admit, that we are either Satan's slaves or Christ's. I can hear the indignant rebuttal; 'I alone decide what I will do. I am the master of my fate, the captain of my soul.' But the Bible makes it plain that there is no third state of existence for man.

"In the spiritual realm, neither ignorance nor deliberate rejection can nullify the fact revealed in God's Word that our lives are dominated either by Satan or by Christ."[20]

Dave Hunt - *The Seduction of Christianity.*

"There are two spiritual beings – the almighty God and Satan – in conflict with each other, and man is the prize in this battle. God has all power, but He will not violate the free will He has given man: We must choose whom we will serve. Satan's weapon to get man to opt for his side is the lie that apart from God we can awaken an infinite potential that lies within each of us."[21]

Paul Barnett - *The Message of Second Corinthians.*

"Humanity has, in reality, been caught up in the cosmic and supernatural uprising of Satan against the one true and living God. Thus mankind is said to be the 'the children of the devil' or of 'the evil one.' John wrote that the 'whole world lies in the evil one,' the imagery suggesting that the human race lies helpless in the coils of a huge serpent. The evil one is also said to be 'in the world,' that is, inhabiting and controlling the minds of all people everywhere."[22]

Russell Kelfer - "Decisions, Decisions, Decisions."

"Satan's story to Eve in Genesis 3, and to Jesus in Matthew 4, was that you can live independently of God, that you can be your own god, set your own standards, let circumstances dictate your decision. BUT IT IS A LIE. Either God controls your life by your choosing to let Him, or Satan controls your life by your choosing (either by design or default) to let him. You and I were designed by God to be ruled by a spirit. Our choice is not whether or not to be ruled, but rather, by which spirit we will be ruled!"[23]

Ian Thomas - *Mystery of Godliness.*

"In the absence of the Holy Spirit instructing and controlling his mind and his emotions and his will with Truth, Satan, who is the father of lies, invaded man, usurped the sovereignty of God, and introduced this evil agency to pollute, corrupt, abuse and misuse his soul and so to twist and bend his will that the behavior mechanism in man, designed by God to be the means whereby he should bear the divine image, was prostituted by the devil to become the means whereby man would bear the satanic image, for 'He that committeth sin is of devil...' (I John 3:8 ... takes his character from the evil one.)"[24]

"The first man, Adam, not only lost the Life of God, and ceased to be in the image of God, but his whole personality became available to the devil, to be exploited by him, producing a race of men whose ungodly behavior...is a demonstration of 'the mystery of iniquity'."[25]

"As godliness is the direct and exclusive consequence of God's activity, and God's capacity to reproduce Himself in you, so all ungodliness is the direct and exclusive consequence of Satan's activity, and of his capacity to reproduce the devil in you! ...iniquity is no more the consequence of your capacity to imitate the devil, than godliness is the consequence of your capacity to imitate God. You cannot begin to understand the mystery of godliness without beginning to understand the mystery of iniquity, because the principles involved are identical! When you act in obedience to the Truth, the Truth behaves, producing godliness; when you act in obedience to the lie, the lie behaves, producing iniquity![26]

"As God is the Author of Truth, so the devil is the author of deception; he is the big lie!"[27]

61

Theological quotations do not of themselves establish the veracity of any point, for they are indeed the opinions of men. But when these statements so consistently affirm that which is demanded by logical necessity, and confirm the Biblical documentation which is the strongest criteria, being the revelation of God, then the cumulative evidence is hard to deny.

Once again, the importance of understanding the condition of the natural man is essential to a clear understanding of the gospel. It is not that the natural man needs to "change his ways" by moralistic behavior modification, nor does he need to "change his thinking" by becoming better educated in a more accurate epistemological belief-system. The need of the natural man is a "spiritual exchange" whereby the "spirit of error" is exchanged for the "spirit of truth" (I John 4:6), the "spirit of the world" is exchanged for the "Spirit of God" (I Cor. 2:12), and the natural man is converted from "darkness to light, from the dominion of Satan to God" (Acts 26:18). Anything less than this is a religious perversion of the Christian gospel!

5

The Perfect Man

Natural man "in Adam" was in a hopeless and helpless condition. He was alienated from God, and without the indwelling presence of God could not be man as God intended man to be. There was nothing man could do to escape from his spiritual predicament of estrangement from God and behavioral dysfunction. Not resolutions, renunciations, reason or religion could remedy his condition.

The only one who could remedy man's fallen situation was God. God would have to take the initiative if there was to be a remedy to man's problem and a restoration of functional humanity, though He was not necessarily obliged to do so. When God acts He cannot act "out of character." He always acts in accord with His character. He *does* what He *does* because He *is* who He *is*.

God is a just God. He is righteous and true. He must keep His word. He cannot lie (Titus 1:2). He said that the consequences of sin would be death. "In the day that you eat thereof, you shall surely die" (Gen. 2:17). Paul also explained this connection of sin and death when he wrote, "the wages of sin is death" (Rom. 6:23), and "the sting of death is sin" (I Cor. 15:56). God's justice required the forfeiture of His life and the subsequent experience of spiritual death as the consequence of sin.

God is also loving. "God is love" (I John 4:8,16). God is gracious and merciful, and desires to act in the highest good of the other, i.e. His creatures, and particularly mankind. God's love and mercy and graciousness prompted His desire to forgive man.

How could God act consistently with His character of justice and gracious mercy at the same time?

Only God could act to counteract that which Satan had done in man. Only by His omnipotence could He overcome him who has the "power of death, that is the devil" (Heb. 2:14), and set aside the "power of our iniquities" (Isa. 64:7). Only God can forgive sin, because sin is a violation of His character. Only God can set men free to once again be man as God intended man to be. Only God can "save" man.

Only man could take the death consequences of sin. The living God cannot die. The just consequences of death for sin must be taken by mortal man.

Only God can deal with sin. Only man can die.

So to express both His justice and His grace at the same time in remedying man's dilemma, the mediator, the saviour, would of necessity have to be a God-man. As God he could administer His power in overcoming the "works of the devil" (I John 3:8) from whom sin is derived, and thus forgive mankind their sin by His grace. As man the mediatorial saviour could be the recipient of the death consequences of sin and satisfy God just demands.

God's remedial and restorative action on man's behalf required a God-man; one who was both God and man at the same time. The paradoxical antimony of this is soon recognized, for the attributes of deity and the attributes of humanity are mutually exclusive in reference to their functionality.

64

God sent His Son, the second person of the Godhead, to be the saviour and mediator. "God so loved the world that He sent His only begotten Son" (John 3:16). "The Word, who was God, became flesh" (John 1:1,14). God, the Son, who from eternity was the One who expressed God as the "Word," and revealed God visibly as the Divine "image" (Col. 1:15; II Cor. 4:4), became man. "There is one mediator between God and man, the man Christ Jesus" (I Tim. 2:5).

The question might be asked: "Why did God wait so long?" If God had from beginning determined to redeem mankind in accord with His character of love and mercy, why did He put off this redemptive action for thousands of years? God knew what He was going to do, for Jesus was "the Lamb slain before the foundation of the world" (Eph. 1:4; Heb. 4:3; Rev. 13:8). (This action not in historical actuality, but in Divine intent.) So why did God postpone the redemptive work of Christ for several millennia?

When Eve bore her first child she apparently thought that she had borne the "seed" who would crush the head of the serpent. She exclaimed, "I have begotten the manchild of Jehovah" (Gen. 4:1). She thought God's promise of the "seed of the woman bruising the serpent's head" (Gen. 3:15) was being fulfilled. Little did she realize how long it would be before such was enacted.

Why did God not place the cross just outside the gates of the garden of Eden, and begin His remedial and redemptive work at once? Is it really consistent with His love to forestall His divine action on man's behalf for such a long period? Yes it was! A preparatory time was needed. Man needed to learn the consequences of sin, the extent of his sinfulness, his utter helplessness to be man as God intended apart from God. Man needed to learn that God was a "God of His word," whose judgement was indeed just. By his inability to keep the commandments of the Law, man would recognize his insufficiency and depravity, and only then be able to appreciate the salvation that God would make available by His Grace in His Son, Jesus Christ. God pictorially prefigured all that He was going to do in Christ by His typological activity throughout the old covenant. Then "in the fullness of time" (which only God can determine); "God sent forth His Son, born of a woman" (Gal. 4:4).

The great christological passage of Philippians 2:6-8 records that "Christ Jesus, although He existed in the form of God, did not regard equality with God a thing to be grasped, but emptied Himself, taking the form of a bond-servant, being made in the likeness of man. And being found in appearance as a man, He humbled Himself by becoming obedient unto death, even death on a cross." What did Jesus empty Himself of? Did He empty Himself of being God? No, for He could still say, "I and the Father are one" (John 10:30), and that not just in purpose or intent, but in essence of Being. Did He empty Himself of certain divine attributes that were incompatible with humanity, such as omnipotence, omnipresence, omniscience, etc.? No, He did not cease to be wholly God with all of His attributes intact. Did He empty Himself of His glory? No, for John explains that "the Word became flesh, and dwelt among us, and we beheld His glory, glory as of the only begotten from the Father" (John 1:14). Jesus emptied Himself of the divine prerogative of independent exercise of His divine activity. God is independent and autonomous, and self-generates His own activity in accord with His character. Man, on the other hand, is a dependent creature who is always functionally dependent, derivative and contingent upon a spiritual resource for his spiritual condition and behavioral expression. In order to become a man, Jesus did not empty Himself of divinity, but merely deferred the independent, autonomous and self-generative exercise of His divine function, in order to function as a man.

This will become more apparent as we consider how Jesus was the "perfect man," by virtue of His being perfect in being, perfect in behavior and perfect in benefit.

"Perfect in Being"

When the Son became man, how did He avoid that which was predicated to all mankind because of Adam's sin? All men died in Adam (Rom. 5:12,15,17,21; I Cor. 15:22). All men were under condemnation (Rom. 5:16,18). All men were made "sinners" (Rom. 5:19) in their essential spiritual condition and identity. All men were "by nature, children of wrath" (Eph. 2:3), with the "prince of the power of the air, (being) the spirit that was working in these sons of disobedience" (Eph. 2:2), identified with the "disobedience" of Adam (Rom. 5:19).

How could Jesus become a man without partaking of spiritual death, Satanic energizing and the inevitable expression of sinful behavior? If He did not escape the transmission of these consequences of Adam's sin, then He would have been in the same helpless and hopeless plight of all mankind. In that condition He could not have saved Himself or anyone else.

In becoming a man, Jesus did not come into being as a man by the same natural processes of human paternity and maternity, as do the rest of mankind. This does not make Him any less human, for He was "born of a woman" (Gal. 4:4) with direct lineage of physical humanity all the way back to Adam, as the genealogies of the gospel records indicate. Adam was human, but his parentage was of divine creation. Jesus is referred to as the "second Adam" or the "second

67

man" (I Cor. 15:47). Jesus was the second man to be born with only God as His paternal father. Jesus told the Jews that He "proceeded forth and came out of God (*ek theos*)" (John 8:42). Like the first Adam (Gen. 2:7), He came into being with the Spirit of God in His spirit. Thus He was perfect in His spiritual being as a man, for the perfect Spirit of God dwelt in Him from His birth.

This is not to imply that Jesus, the "second Adam," was the same or identical to the first Adam. Adam was a man with the spirit of God's life in the man (Gen. 2:7). Jesus was incarnate deity. He was God, and never ceased to be God, but became man.

The Son of God becoming man was accomplished via the supernatural conception of a child in the womb of Mary. The paternal seed (*sperma*) was not provided by Joseph but by the Holy Spirit. The God-man was the "seed (or progeny) of the woman" (Gen. 3:15), "born of a woman" (Gal. 4:4), without human paternity. Some have speculated that the transmission of the death consequences of Adam (cf. chapter 4) throughout the human race is through the seminal paternal transmission of the human father, but evidence for such is inconclusive. What we do know is that Joseph was not the human paternal father of the baby that was conceived in the womb of Mary, and this was quite unsettling because Joseph and Mary were not yet married. When Mary was advised that she was going to have a child, she asked, "How can this be? I am a virgin." The angel explained that "The Holy Spirit will come upon you." (Luke 1:34,35). Joseph, likewise was told, "Do not be afraid to take Mary as your wife, for that which is conceived in her is of the Holy Spirit" (Matt. 1:20). Jesus was conceived by the supernatural conception of the Holy Spirit, which is often referred to as the "virgin birth," and thus He did not partake of the spiritual and behavioral consequences of death that came upon all natural men because of Adam's sin. This evidences the necessity of understanding and accepting the "virgin birth" or supernatural conception of Jesus Christ, else He could not have been "perfect in being" and the sinless Savior of mankind. To jettison or deny such is to cut the heart out of the gospel.

Born "perfect in being," Jesus was not born "dead in trespasses and sins" (Eph. 2:1,5) as are all natural men, but rather the Spirit of God's Life indwelt His spirit from conception. Jesus did not have the personal resource of death, the "one having the power of death, that is the devil" (Heb. 2:14) operating and energizing within His spirit, as all natural men seem to have from their birth (Eph. 2:2). To His disciples Jesus explained, "The ruler of the world...has nothing in Me" (John 14:30. Jesus was perfect in spiritual being by the presence of the Perfect Spirit of God indwelling the spirit of the man, Christ Jesus.

"Perfect in Behavior"

How did Jesus live the life that He lived? Did He have some additional capabilities since He was God to live life as a man? Did He have something that allowed Him to live perfectly that Christians do not have?

The perfect spiritual condition of the human Jesus gave Him the perfect potential to evidence behaviorally the character of the Perfect One who dwelt in His human spirit. In the behavior mechanism of His soul there was open access for God to function in the behavior of the man, as God intended when He first created man. Jesus did not have the patterned propensities of the "flesh" which have developed in all natural men, who while functioning as "slaves of sin" (John 8:34; Rom. 6:6) form tendencies of selfishness and sinfulness in

69

their behavior patterns. These patterns of behavior were not formed from the earliest years of His life as they are in all natural men, but this does not necessarily mean that Jesus had any resource or capability for behavior that other men (that is Christian persons) do not have.

Although He was God, He did not function as God during His life and redemptive mission on earth. God functions by the independent, autonomous and self-generated activity of His own Being and character. Man is a dependent creature who functions only and always by derivative and contingent receptivity from a spiritual resource. Although Jesus could *be* God and *be* man at the same time, He could not *function* as God and *function* as man at the same time. He could not *behave* as God and *behave* as man simultaneously. This is why He "emptied Himself" (Phil. 2:7) of the prerogatives of divine function, determining not to exercise those infinite capabilities independently. In order to become fully man He had to become functionally subordinate and thus to function, act and behave as a man, who by receptive derivation and dependency would allow the indwelling Father and Spirit to function as God in the man.

In conjunction with all human beings Jesus had freedom of choice. He had the volitional option as to whether He would allow the perfection of spiritual being which indwelt Him to be experientially manifested in His behavior of soul and body as a man. Although He was never "in the flesh" (Rom. 8:9) entrapped by fleshly tendencies, He was nevertheless tempted to choose to engage in fleshly activities. He was "tempted in all points as we are, yet without sin" (Heb. 4:15).

The question is often asked, "Could Jesus have sinned when He was tempted?" In theological terminology this is the issue of the impeccability of Jesus. James explains that "God cannot be tempted by evil..." (James 1:13). Some argue therefore that since Jesus was God He could not be tempted to evil. What they are forgetting is that although Jesus was indeed God, never less than God, He was functioning behaviorally as a man. It was not as God that He was tempted, but as a man. W. Ian Thomas explains,

> "It is no explanation to suggest that though *tempted*, the Lord Jesus Christ was not tempted with *evil*...for the statement 'yet without sin' clearly indicates that the nature of the temptation was such that it would have led to sin had it not been resisted. ...inherent in His willingness to be made man, was the willingness of the Lord Jesus Christ to be made subject to temptation,... ...inherent in man's capacity to be godly is man's capacity to sin."[1]

It is of no value to speculate on such hypothetical questions as: "What would have happened if Jesus had opted to sin?" "Did God have any other options by which to save mankind?" These are questions that have no answers.

In spite of the temptations to choose to engage in behavior that was less than perfect and not derived from God, Jesus did not so choose and did not sin. The Scriptural record is abundantly clear that Jesus was "without sin" (Heb. 4:15). "In Him there was no sin" (I John 3:5). He "knew no sin" (II Cor. 5:21), and "committed no sin, nor was any deceit found in His mouth" (I Peter 2:22). Jesus Himself could ask His contemporaries, "Which of you convicts Me of sin?" (John 8:46), and no one could do so. He was a "high priest, holy, innocent, undefiled, separated from sinners" (Heb. 7:26), who "offered Himself without blemish" (Heb. 9:14), "a lamb unblemished and spotless" (I Peter 1:19).

Jesus did not sin, but the mere avoidance of sin is not necessarily "perfect behavior." To avoid sin may be to simply do nothing at all, but that too might be the sin of omission.

Anyone who observes the recorded life of Jesus cannot conclude that He was lethargic or passive. He was very active, and the entirety of His activity was the expression of "perfect behavior." Perfect behavior is only the result of a choice which allows the perfect God within a man to express His perfect character perfectly in the behavior of a man. When such "perfect behavior" is expressed in a man, God is "well pleased," and God proclaims such divine pleasure concerning the behavior of Jesus Christ both at His baptism (Matt. 3:17) and at His transfiguration (Matt. 17:5). God is only well pleased and glorified by the manifestation of His own perfect character. Jesus knew that this was the basis of His human functioning, for He asserts, "I always do the things that are pleasing to Him" (John 8:29).

Jesus exercised His freedom of choice to allow the perfect God to function perfectly within the man for every moment in time for thirty-three years. He always chose to let God function through His humanity. Such receptivity of God's activity is the way that man was designed by God to function.

Repeatedly Jesus explained the *modus operandi* of His behavior to those who observed what He said and what He did. "The Son can do nothing of Himself; ...the Father shows the Son all things that He Himself is doing" (John 5:19,20). "I can do nothing on My own initiative. As I hear, I judge" (John 5:30). "I did not speak on My own initiative, but the Father Himself has given Me...what to say, and what to speak" (John 12:49). "The words that I say to you I do not speak on My own initiative, but the Father abiding in Me does His works" (John 14:10). Jesus did not function by His rightful divine initiative of independent, autonomous and self-generative function. As a man He was receptive to the divine activity that His indwelling Father desired to express through Him. Functioning as a man He derived all of His behavior from God, contingent upon the Father in the dependency of functionally subordinate faith.

Thus functioning as God intended man to function, Jesus was imaging the character of God in all that He did. "When you see Me, you see God in action." "He who beholds Me, beholds Him who sent Me" (John 12:45). The invisible character of God was perfectly "imaged" in the visible perfect behavior of a man, the Perfect Man, Jesus Christ, who was but man as God intended man to be – normally functional humanity. Christ was, and is, "the image of God" (Col. 1:15: II Cor. 4:4); the fullness of deity dwelling in bodily form (Col. 2:10), but the basis of His human functionality is intended to be the basis of the function of all mankind.

Though Jesus thoroughly explains that "the Father abiding in Me does His works" (John 14:10), and that He just participates in "whatever the Father does" (John 5:19), some still question whether the independent initiative of divine action was necessitated for Jesus to work miracles. Peter explains in the first sermon of the church that Jesus was "a man attested to you by God with miracles and wonders and signs which God performed through Him" (Acts 2:22). How did Jesus perform the miracles? As a man He was receptive to the supernatural activity of God operative through Him. Thus it is that Peter and Paul and others throughout Christian history have been able to express the supernatural work of God also.

In light of the human functionality of "the man, Christ Jesus," who demonstrated "perfect behavior" by His receptivity of divine activity, why is it then that Christians are so keen to demur and to claim that "Jesus could live like He did because He was God, but we are just human." No! Jesus was a man who lived like He did because He chose in faith to allow the Father who indwelt Him to act through Him.

Christians who have become "partakers of the divine nature" (II Peter 1:4) have the same indwelling spiritual resource, that they might choose in faith to allow the indwelling Christ to express His character and activity through them, to the glory of God. We cannot cop out by using the excuse of the inadequacy of mere humanity, for it was in just such humanity that Jesus exhibited "perfect behavior."

Though "perfect in being" and "perfect in behavior," Jesus still needed to be "made perfect." In fact, at the risk of being misunderstood, I might assert that if Jesus were merely "perfect in being" and "perfect in behavior," the world would have been better off without Him. Why? Because such a matchless example would have condemned us all the more. No other man could be born as He was born, "perfect in being," and therefore no other man could have behaved as He behaved, "perfect in behavior." Such incapability would have been frustratingly condemnable. But Jesus did not come to condemn us by a matchless example; He came to become condemnation for us as a vicarious sacrifice. Therein He was "made perfect" in the obedience of the things which He suffered (Heb. 5:8,9). "Jesus, by the suffering of death...was perfected as the author of our salvation through sufferings" (Heb. 2:8,9).

"Perfect in Benefit"

The perfect purpose of God in having His Son become man was that He might provide the "perfect benefit" for all of mankind in the remedial and restorative activity of the Messiah. The remedial action is observed in the death of Jesus Christ whereby He takes the death consequences of the sin of mankind upon Himself. The restorative action is the result of the resurrection of Christ whereby the life of God is once again made available to mankind.

Some have asked, "Why did Jesus have to die?" It is not that death is intrinsic to humanity, for Adam could have eaten from the "tree of life" and "lived forever" (Gen. 3:22). Human death is the consequence of sin (Gen. 2:17). But Jesus was "without sin" (Heb. 4:15), so why did He have to die? He became a man in order to die! He "came to give His life a ransom for many" (Matt. 20:28). God sent His Son "in the likeness of sinful flesh," so that He might be "an offering for sin" (Rom. 8:3). He came to earth as a man to assume the death consequences of the human race. In His death He incurred all of the death consequences that had occurred in Adam and which were thus transmitted to all mankind, in order to reverse those consequences and allow for spiritual re-creation that man might function as God intended man to function.

Jesus, who "knew no sin, was made to be sin on our behalf" (II Cor. 5:21). The man, Christ Jesus, was undeserving of any death consequences since He was "perfect in being" and "perfect in behavior." It was the sin of all mankind that was imputed to Jesus Christ that He might bear the death consequences thereof. It was not His sin but our sin that made Him liable to death. "Christ died for sins,...the just for the unjust" (I Peter 3:18).

It is interesting to note the contrast between the first man, Adam, and the second man, Jesus Christ. Both faced a human choice at the site of a tree. Adam made a choice of "disobedience" (Rom. 5:19) at the "tree of the knowledge of good and evil" (Gen. 2:17; 3:3-6, and as a consequence all men "were made sinners" (Rom. 5:19), (designating their spiritual condition and identity), and condemned to partake of the death consequences (Rom. 5:12,14,17) of sin. Jesus Christ made a

75

choice of "obedience" (Rom. 5:19), "learning obedience through the things which He suffered" (Heb. 5:8), "becoming obedient to the point of death, even death on a cross" (Phil. 2:8). It was at that "tree" of the cross (Acts 5:30; Gal. 3:13) that Jesus was "made sin" (II Cor. 5:21). The sin of the entire human race was imputed to Him. The composite quantification and qualification of all sin was invested in Him. As a sinless man He became the diabolic personification of all sin contrary to the character of God. Vicariously He became the sinless substitutionary sacrifice to satisfy the just consequences of death for sin.

The totality of the death consequences which occurred in Adam were incurred by Jesus Christ: the personal resource of death, the prevailing ramifications of death, and the perpetual representation of death.[2]

The "prevailing ramifications" of death are most evident, for as the "god of this world" (II Cor. 4:4) came against Jesus, personally and directly in the temptations in the wilderness, and through his religious agents in Judaism, Jesus was physically crucified by "death on a cross" (Phil. 2:8). The physical death of Jesus Christ was empirically observed and is historically verifiable. The gory details of death by crucifixion have adequately been explained by many authors.

How the "personal resource" of death was imputed to Jesus on the cross is more difficult to understand. If Jesus took all the death consequences for man, then He not only took upon Himself physical death but also spiritual death, for that is the first aspect of death that occurred in Adam (Gen. 2:17). The theologians of early Christianity often explained that "the unassumed is the unrestored," implying that if Jesus did not assume all of the human death consequences, then the remedial action necessary for the restoration of God's life in man would be inadequate. Jesus seems to have assumed spiritual death when He cried out from the cross, 'My God, My God, Why hast Thou forsaken Me?" (Matt 27:46; Mark 15:34), and "gave up His spirit" (Matt. 27:50; John 19:30). He experienced the separation from and absence of the life of God in the man, which is spiritual death. As a derivative creature, man can never be an autonomous, independent void. Spiritual death is not annihilation or mere cessation. Jesus was "made to be sin" (II Cor. 5:21), and the source of all sin is in Satan (I John 3:8). Could it be that the "spirit" (Eph. 2:2), the "one having the power of death, that is the devil" (Heb. 2:14), actually invaded the spirit of the man, Christ Jesus, at that last moment of His pre-crucifixion existence, and entered into the one man he had never been able to get into? If so, Jesus became the personification of all sin, even of Satan himself, and God poured out His wrath, the judgment of sin, on all that was contrary to His character. This might also explain the suddenness of Jesus' physical death, which surprised the observers who knew that crucifixion was a slow and agonizing process of death (John 19:33). Could it be that in giving up His spirit (Mark 15:37; Luke 23:46) He "laid down His own life" (John 10:17,18) in physical death so as to disallow any Satanic activity in the behavior of His soul and body which would have contravened the sinless sacrifice? "The body without the spirit is dead" (James 2:26). These latter questions are indeed speculative conjectures, but the reality of the assumption of spiritual death by Jesus must not be overlooked.

The extent to which Jesus experienced the "perpetual representation" of the death consequences of man's sin is even more difficult to explain. The Apostle's Creed formulated early in Christian history indicates that Jesus "descended into hell." The scriptural record reports that Jesus "descended into the lower parts of the earth" (Eph. 4:9) and "preached to the spirits in prison" (I Pet. 3:19), "even to those who are dead" (I Pet. 4:6), and "His soul was not abandoned to Hades" (Acts 2:27,31). Though we could wish for more details, they are not provided. In some manner that is beyond human explanation, Jesus experienced the qualitative, or even quantitative, everlastingness of death in the midst of His physical death. The temporal factors of timing, whether this was during the three hours of darkness or during the three days of physical death cannot be ascertained and need not be, for with God "a day is as a thousand years" (II Pet. 3:8), and thus Jesus could have experienced the everlastingness of death within any period of time.

In His death on the cross Jesus accomplished what the Father had given Him to do. It was a victory cry that He issued from the cross, "It is finished!" It was certainly not a cry of defeat about having come to an untimely end, whereby the mission was aborted. The Greek word *tetelestai* that Jesus exclaimed was derived from the word *telos,* meaning "end." Jesus was declaring that the perfect end-objective of God for man was accomplished. The resurrection, Pentecostal outpouring, and even the consummation of His return, though not yet historically enacted, were inevitable consequential outworkings of the remedial action that was achieved in His death. Death and sin were defeated. "Mission accomplished!" "Paid in full!" "It is finished!" Indeed it was, for "the Son of God appeared for this purpose, that He might destroy the works of the devil" (I John 3:8), and "through death render powerless the one having the power of death, that is the devil" (Heb. 2:14).

For the man, Christ Jesus, who was sinless, yea perfect, "it was impossible for Him to be held in death's power" (Acts 2:24), and "His flesh did not suffer decay" (Acts 2:27,31; 13:35). He had no personal sin, by the consequence of which

78

"the one having the power of death, that is the devil" (Heb. 2:14) could hold Him. He thus was resurrected unto life out of death.

By the resurrection of Jesus Christ the life of God was restored for the first time to a man who had experienced spiritual death. The resurrection of Jesus had been foretold by David (Psalm 16:10; Acts 2:31; 13:35), who also indicated that the resurrection was a type of birth (Psalm 2:7; Acts 13:33; Heb. 5:5), as the Perfect Man was restored to life out of death. Jesus was the "first-born from the dead" (Col. 1:18; Rev. 1:5). This cannot mean that He was the first man to be restored to physical life out of physical death (Luke 7:15; John 11:44), but the first man to have experienced spiritual death and then to be restored to spiritual life. Do not think that Jesus was "born again" in the same way that Christians are, for we fallen human beings were spiritually dead as "sinners" deserving such consequence, whereas Jesus was "made sin" and His death was an undeserved consequence of our sin. His resurrection was accomplished by virtue of His own sinlessness and the power of God (Eph. 1:19,20) whereby He had the power to "take it up again" (John 10:17,18), whereas our restoration to life is accomplished only by virtue of His sacrificial death on our behalf, and the availability of His resurrection-life poured out by the Spirit of Christ at Pentecost.

By His resurrection Jesus became the "first-fruits of those who are asleep" (I Cor. 15:20,23), and "the first born among many brethren" (Rom. 8:29), who could in similar manner based on the prototypical resurrection/birth of Jesus Christ be restored to spiritual life out of spiritual death by receiving His life. "By reason of His resurrection from the dead, He was the first to proclaim light both to Jew and Gentile" (Acts 26:23). Having experienced life out of death, Jesus proclaimed the availability to all men of experiencing spiritual "life out of death" (John 5:24; I John 3:14), being "raised to newness of life" (Rom. 6:4) as they are "raised up with Christ" (Col. 2:12; 3:1) by the receptivity of His resurrection-life.

By His resurrection "the last Adam became a life-giving spirit" (I Cor. 15:45) making available His life (John 11:25; 14:6) to restore the Life of God to mankind and re-create man as a "new man" (II Cor. 5:17; Eph. 4:24; Col. 3:10). We can be "born again to a living hope through the resurrection of Jesus Christ from the dead" (I Peter 1:3).

Only by His being "perfect in being" (supernaturally conceived with God as His father and indwelt by the Spirit of God) could Jesus have been "perfect in behavior" (allowing the character of God to be expressed perfectly at every moment in time for thirty-three years). Only as He was "perfect in behavior" (receptive by faith to let God act through Him) could Jesus have been "perfect in benefit" (taking the death consequences of all mankind in order to give us His life). His sinless submission made His sacrifice sufficient in order to restore the life of God to man. He was indeed the "Perfect Man," and because He was "Man as God intended Man to be," we can be man as God intended man to be by His life functioning in us, deity within humanity, Christ within the Christian.

6

The Restoration of Man

The work of Jesus Christ is based upon the person of Jesus Christ. His sinless spiritual condition and behavioral expression made His sacrifice sufficient for mankind. He could be "perfect in benefit" because He was "perfect in being" and "perfect in behavior."

Theological considerations must avoid positing Christ's work only in terms of "benefits," however. To do so creates an overly objectified disjuncture of the work of Jesus Christ from the living person of Jesus Christ. His work must not be divorced from His person, and reduced into static commodities or "benefits" to mankind. The effects or benefits of the work of Jesus Christ are encompassed in His Being. The ontological dynamic of the work of Christ must be recognized. He *did* what He *did*, and *does* what He *does*, because He *is* who He *is*. All of His acts are inherent in His Being.

The work of Jesus Christ is usually referred to in theological terminology as the "atonement." The first known usage of this word in the English vocabulary of theology dates back to the sixteenth century, when it was used as a hyphenated conjunction of the two words "at-onement." William Tyndale used the word within his English translation of 1526. The *Authorized Version*, also known as the *King James Version*, published in 1611, made repeated usage of the word "atonement" to translate the Hebrew word *kapar* (covering), translating *Yom Kippur* (Day of Coverings) as "Day of Atonement." The Greek word *katallage* in Rom. 5:11 was also translated as "atonement" in the Authorized Version, whereas other usages of the same word were translated as "reconciliation."

The divine action of God in His Son Jesus Christ was initiated out of His own character of love and grace. Mankind was incapable of taking any action that could remedy his helpless and hopeless predicament of sin and death. "God so loved the world that he gave His only begotten Son" (John 3:16). "He loved us and sent His Son" (I John 4:9,10), "demonstrating His love for us, in that while we were yet sinners, Christ died for us" (Rom. 5:8). The "gift of grace" came through Jesus Christ (Rom. 5:12,15). "We are justified as a gift, by His grace through the redemption which is in Christ Jesus" (Rom. 3:24).

The action of God in His Son, Jesus Christ, is such a unique, one-of-a-kind, Divine reality, that it is beyond human explanation. Attempts to explain it in human language must employ inadequate human images and concepts which serve as anthropocentric representations and analogies of what God has done. Even the human language used in the Bible must utilize such terminology for explanation. Analogical images such as blood, ransom and legal offense, for example, convey certain concepts or ideas to the human mind in order to assist our understanding of the work of Christ.

The whole complement of the images and concepts that are employed within the inspired Scriptures to explain what Christ came to do must be held together in a collective composite if we are to maintain a theological understanding that is as full and accurate as man is capable of grasping. The whole picture must be kept in perspective, avoiding the myopic misunderstanding that results from considering only a piece or two of the puzzle. This has been one of the theological pitfalls throughout the history of Christian theology. There has been a tendency to focus on a particular image or concept of Christ's work, to the exclusion, diminishing or neglect of other analogies, which results in an unbalanced theological view of atonement with varying misemphases. Another pitfall has been the careless mixing and merging of metaphors which creates mystical misunderstandings and confusions.

In an attempt to consider the primary images and analogies that the Bible uses to explain the work of Jesus, we will note the concepts that are introduced by those images and consequent models that utilize some of those concepts.

Concepts

The images portrayed by the Scriptures introduce us to certain concepts through which we might understand God's action in His Son, Jesus Christ. The concepts are further amplified by the vocabulary of various biblical and theological terms. The concepts which are objective to man will be considered first, to be followed by the subjective concepts which are effected within man.

The Liberational Concept. The fall of mankind into sin and death necessarily allowed dependent and contingent mankind to be held by another spiritual authority other than God, i.e. the Satanic slave-master. To resolve man's enslavement, the work of God in Christ would need to deliver, rescue and liberate man from his spiritual bondage and slavery.

Having fallen under "the dominion of Satan" (Acts 26:18) in "the domain of darkness" (Col. 1:13), mankind was in "the bondage of iniquity" (Acts 8:23) and "the elemental things of the world" (Gal. 4:3), "bound" under the Law (Rom. 7:6). Enslaved to "sin" (Rom. 6:6,17), to "impurity and lawlessness" (Rom. 6:19), to "fear and death" (Rom. 8:15; Heb. 2:15), mankind was a "host of captives" (Luke 4:18; Eph. 4:8), "held captive by the devil to do his will" (II Tim. 2:26).

Jesus Christ was the Liberator who would "release the captives" (Luke 4:18) "from the Law" (Rom. 7:2,6) and "from their sins" (Rev. 1:5). He came to "deliver men from the domain of darkness" (Col. 1:13), "from this present evil age" (Gal. 1:4), from "the slavery brought on by the fear of death" (Heb. 2:15), and "from every evil deed" (II Tim. 4:18). As man's Deliverer, He came to "set free those who are downtrodden" (Luke 4:18), to set them "free from the Law" (Rom. 7:3-6) and "from the law of sin and death" (Rom. 8:2). "If the Son shall set you free, you shall be free indeed" (John 8:36), in "the freedom of the glory of the children of God" (Rom. 8:21). "It was for freedom that Christ set us free" (Gal. 5:1), and Christians must "act as free men" (I Peter 2:16). "Where the Spirit of the Lord is there is liberty" (II Cor. 3:17), and Christians are to live by the "perfect law of liberty" (James 1:25; 2:12).

Several biblical terms convey the meaning of release, deliverance and setting free. The Greek word *lutroo*, which is often translated "redemption" throughout the New Testament, means "to loose, to set free, to deliver." Christians are "redeemed from their transgressions" (Heb. 9:15) and "from every lawless deed" (Titus 2:14). The Greek word *aphiemi* is often translated as "forgiveness" in the New Testament, and means "to dismiss" or "to release" from sins (Eph. 1:7; Col. 1:14). The word which is translated "salvation," from the Greek word *soteria,* can also mean "to make safe" by delivering from evil.

The Legal and Penal Concept. Since God is pictured as "the Judge of all" (Heb. 12:23) who "will judge His people" (Heb. 10:30), "the living and the dead" (I Pet. 4:5), the legal or penal concept wherein God reacts to man's sin in a judicial context is evident through many biblical images.

The "offense of Adam" (Rom. 5:14) was a "transgression" (Rom. 5:15-19) of God's intent for man, which affected the entire human race in spiritual solidarity with Adam. All men were "dead in their transgressions" (Eph. 2:5; Col. 2:13), "dead in trespasses and sins" (Eph. 2:1). "Condemnation came upon all men" (Rom. 5:16,18), and all were made liable to "the penalty of eternal destruction" (II Thess. 1:9), the "eternal punishment" (Matt. 25:46) of "fire" (Jude 1:7) at "the day of judgment" (II Peter 2:9). God "has fixed a day when He shall judge the world in righteousness, through a Man" (Acts 17:31), His Son, Jesus Christ. There will be "retribution to those who do not know God and obey the gospel of Jesus Christ" (II Thess. 1:8). There is no doubt that the Bible uses legal and penal imagery to describe the relation of God to fallen mankind.

Jesus Christ is represented as willing to take the "death penalty" on behalf of the human race, effecting the "forgiveness of sins" (Acts 10:43; 26:18; Col. 1:14), "the forgiveness of our trespasses" (Eph. 1:7). He "put away sin by the sacrifice of Himself" (Heb. 9:26). Many times throughout the New Testament, the Greek words *dikaioo* and *dikaioma* are translated as "to justify" and "justification." God in Christ "justifies the ungodly" (Rom. 4:5), for they are "justified in His blood" (Rom. 5:9) resulting in "justification of life to all men" (Rom. 5:18). The Greek term was indeed used as a legal term, but not exclusively (as will be noted later). When so used it often referred to the idea of acquittal, whereby a verdict of "not guilty" or "right-standing" before the judge or the law was issued, a declaration of rightness. The legal and penal consequences of sin were resolved by Jesus Christ.

The Purificational Concept. Before the purity of God's character of absolute holiness, man's sin is an impurity and uncleanness. The work of Jesus Christ serves to purify the condition of fallen mankind.

The prophets indicate that the sins of fallen mankind are "red like crimson" (Isa. 1:18), serving as "the stain of iniquity" (Jer. 2:22). Ontologically deriving their character from the Evil One, "God gave them over in the lusts of their hearts to impurity" (Rom. 1:24), and they became "slaves to impurity" (Rom. 6:19). "No impure person has an inheritance in the kingdom of Christ and God" (Eph. 5:5).

Christ's atoning work allows fallen mankind to "wash their robes and make them white in the blood of the Lamb" (Rev. 7:14). Christians are those who are "washed and sanctified" (I Cor. 6:11), having "washed away their sins" (Acts 22:16) in the "washing of regeneration" (Titus 3:5). The "blood of Christ cleanses our conscience from dead works" (Heb. 9:14); our hearts are "cleansed by faith" (Acts 15:9), and we can continue to be "cleansed from all unrighteousness" (I John 1:9). Jesus has effected "purification of sins" (Heb. 1:3; II Pet. 1:9), having "purified for Himself a people for His own possession" (Titus 2:14) as they "in obedience to the truth purify their souls" (I Pet. 1:22). Christ's work was a cleansing, washing and purifying action.

The Thanatological Concept. The Greek word for "death" is *thanatos*. From the very commencement of man's function as a choosing creature, God explained that the consequence of sin would involve death. "In the day that you eat thereof, you shall surely die" (Gen. 2:17). "The wages of sin is death" (Rom. 6:23). "Death spread to all men" (Rom. 5:12) by their spiritual solidarity with Adam and his choice of sin. "In Adam all die" (I Cor. 15:22) and are "excluded from the life of God" (Eph. 4:18). The death consequences that came upon fallen mankind began with the absence of God's life in the spirit, but must be understood as an ontological connection with "the one having the power of death, that is the devil" (Heb. 2:14). Spiritual death involves the presence of the personal resource of death, i.e. Satan, whose activity generates the prevailing ramifications of behavioral death and physical death, which if unabated will lead to the perpetual representation of everlasting death. (See chapters on "The Fall of Man" and "The End of Man")

The consequence of death as a result of man's sin is not just a penal consequence of the "death penalty." Life is an inherent feature of the character of God. "The Father has life in Himself" (John 5:26). As all sin is contrary to His character, the incongruity demands a separation and privation of His presence and character expression, logically demanding the opposite spiritual resource of the diabolic source of death.

Jesus Christ came to incur the death consequences that had occurred in Adam. As God, He could not die, but as man he could assume those death consequences. As a derivative and contingent man, He submitted voluntarily and vicariously to death, which included physical, spiritual and everlasting expressions thereof. "Christ died for us" (Rom. 5:8), the "ungodly" (Rom. 5:6). "Christ died for our sins according to the Scriptures" (I Cor. 15:3), "once and for all" (Rom. 6:10; I Pet. 3:18).

The image of "blood" is often used within the New Testament to refer to the death of Christ. His blood has no magical or mystical efficacy in itself, so all references to His "shed blood" should be interpreted as indicating the thanatological concept of death. "Redemption through His blood" (Eph. 1:7), "justification by His blood" (Rom. 5:9), "propitiation in His blood" (Rom. 3:25), "forgiveness by His blood" (Heb. 9:22), and the "cleansing of sin by His blood" (I John 1:7) should all be understood as the consequences of His taking death for mankind.

Likewise, the "cross" should not be construed as an object that conveys spiritual benefits. The cross was a death instrument. References to the "cross of Christ" (I Cor. 1:17; Col. 1:20) and His crucifixion direct our attention to the thanatological concept of His death on our behalf. We "boast in the cross" (Gal. 6:14) and "preach Christ crucified" (I Cor. 1:23) because Jesus took our death consequences.

There is a subjective aspect to the thanatological concept of death, for when Jesus died He effected a spiritual solidarity with all who would receive Him and His death on their behalf. The old spiritual identity of the unregenerate is regarded as having been put to death in identification with the death of Christ. When He died, we died. He died for us and as us. "The One died for all, therefore all died" (II Cor. 5:14). "Our old self was crucified with Him" (Rom. 6:6). "We have died with Christ" (Rom. 6:8; Col. 2:20). "I have been crucified with Christ" (Gal. 2:20)

The Sacrificial Concept. Immediately after the sin of Adam, God instituted a sacrificial system whereby man could view the consequences of his sin. Cain and Abel, the first sons of Adam and Eve, "brought offerings" (Gen. 4:3,4), but "Abel offered a better sacrifice than Cain" (Heb. 11:4). The sacrifices were a pictorial prefiguring of what would be required to deal with man's sin. Inherent in the concept of sacrifice is the idea of (1) cost, the forfeiture and relinquishment of something of value, a price to be paid, and (2) the idea of substitution, the vicarious replacement of the one having to die, a transference of liability from the offerer to the living object being sacrificed.

"Christ gave Himself up for us, an offering and a sacrifice to God" (Eph. 5:2). He became the "Passover sacrifice" (I Cor. 5:7), who "offered one sacrifice for sins for all time" (Heb. 10:12) and "put away sin by the sacrifice of Himself" (Heb. 9:26). He is "the Lamb of God who takes away the sin of the world" (John 1:29), and we are "sanctified through the offering of the body of Jesus" (Heb. 10:10) and by His "sprinkled blood" (Heb. 12:24).

The substitutional element of His sacrifice is evident in that "the Lord has caused the iniquity of us all to fall on Him" (Isa. 53:6). "While we were yet sinners Christ died for us" (Rom. 5:8) and "became a curse for us" (Gal. 3:13). "He bore our sins in His body on the tree" (I Pet. 2:24), and "died, the just for the unjust, that He might bring us to God" (I Pet. 3:18). The sacrificial concept of Christ's work was pre-figured in the old covenant and fulfilled in the enactment of the new covenant.

The Covenantal Concept. The agreement between God and man always necessitated the activity of God being received by man's faith. Fallen mankind had "broken the covenant" (Isa. 33:8), as had the specific people (Jer. 11:10) God had selected for the prefiguring of His intent in His Son, Jesus Christ. This necessitated a "new covenant" (Jer. 31:31) between God and man.

The work of Jesus Christ effects that "new covenant" (Heb. 9:15). He is "the mediator of a new covenant" (Heb. 12:24), the "guarantee of a better covenant" (Heb. 7:22). As covenants between men were usually sealed with a blood sacrifice to represent the consequences of breaking the covenant, the death of Jesus served as the "blood of the covenant" (Heb. 10:29; 13:20), whereby He established a "new covenant in His blood" (Matt. 26:28; I Cor. 11:25). The sacrificial concept and the covenantal concept are thus inexorably interconnected.

The Economical Concept. The sin of mankind is represented as creating a situation of indebtedness before God which requires compensation and reparation. There is a price to be paid, a "certificate of debt consisting of decrees against us" (Col. 2:14). Some of the early Christian writers (ex. Origin, Gregory of Nyssa) engaged in wild speculation that the devil had kidnapped the human race, holding them as hostages, and God was paying off the devil by deceptively trading Jesus as a "ransom" for mankind. Far be it from the character of God to engage in such deceit, or to be indebted to the devil.

The image of "ransom" carries with it the idea of release from bondage in exchange for a payment. Mankind was indeed in bondage to sin, needing to be released (liberational concept). "The Son of Man came to give His life a ransom for many" (Matt. 20:28; Mark 10:45), and "gave Himself as a ransom for all" (I Tim. 2:6). We were "bought with a price" (I Cor. 6:19,20; 7:23), "purchased with His blood" (Acts 20:28).

The terminology of "redemption" expresses this economical, commercial or financial concept, for the Greek word *exagorazo* means "to buy out of the market place," and the word *apolutrosis* can mean "to release upon payment of a ransom." Both of these words are translated "redeem" in the New Testament; note Gal. 3:13 and Eph. 1:7 respectively.

The Transactional Concept. Man's sin required that a transaction take place which would satisfy God. The image of

Divine satisfaction has led to several different interpretations. Some have understood that God demanded satisfaction of His legal demands or satisfaction of His justice (legal or penal concept), or the satisfaction of a compensatory payment (economical concept). Others have explained that God's wrath toward sin must be satisfied. God is indeed "jealous" of His character (Exod. 20:5; 34:14; Deut. 4:24; Josh. 24:19; Nahum 1:2). "The wrath of God is revealed from heaven against all ungodliness and unrighteousness of men" (Rom. 1:18), and "comes upon the sons of disobedience" (Eph. 5:6) who "do not obey the Son" (John 3:36). We must, however, beware of pushing this image into crude ideas of God's capricious and arbitrary anger, whereby He is cast as an offended deity who suffered a personal affront because of the offense against His honor or dignity, and needs to be placated, pacified, mollified or soothed by the smoothing of His ruffled feathers.

The satisfaction that God requires is consistency with His character. That would require the severing of the ontological connection of mankind with evil in order to provide ontological union between God and man again. In His death Jesus Christ vicariously lived out that ontological break, exclaiming, "My God, My God, why have You forsaken Me?" (Ps. 22:1; Matt. 27:46; Mark 15:34), and through His resurrection restored "the provision of the Spirit" (Phil. 1:19) so that the character of God might be operative in man.

God is satisfied with what Christ has accomplished (John 4:34; 5:36; 17:4; 19:28) to alleviate the contrariety of his character through ontological derivation from the Evil One, and to bring Him pleasure by the faithful ontological receptivity of His character (Heb. 11:6). "Justified by His blood, we shall be saved from the wrath of God through Him" (Jesus Christ) (Rom. 5:9).

The theological terms employed to express this Divine satisfaction in the work of Jesus Christ are the words "propitiation" and "expiation." Much argumentation has transpired as to which of these words best expresses the Greek word *hilaskomai*. "God sent His Son to be the propitiation/expiation for our sins" (I John 4:10; 2:1,2; Heb. 2:17), and "displayed Him publicly as a propitiation/ expiation in His blood" (Rom. 3:25).

The Triumphal Concept. Throughout the Scriptures there is the image of a cosmic conflict between God and Satan, between good and evil. This is never portrayed as a dualism of equal powers, however, since God is omnipotent. "There was war in heaven" (Rev. 12:7) that caused "enmity between the serpent and the seed of woman" (Gen. 3:15), requiring that "the ruler of this world be cast out" (John 12:31).

The work of Christ accomplished victory over Satan. "He disarmed the rulers and authorities, having triumphed over them" (Col. 2:15). He is "victorious over the beast" (Rev. 15:2). "The Son of God appeared that He might destroy the works of the devil" (I John 3:8), and "through death He rendered powerless the one having the power of death, that is the devil" (Heb. 2:14). The Lion (Rev. 5:5) who is the Lamb (Rev. 17:14) has "overcome the world" (John 16:33) and the "Evil One" (I John 2:14). "He leads justice to victory" (Matt. 12:20). "Thanks be to God who gives us the victory through Jesus Christ" (I Cor. 15:57).

In addition to the above stated objective concepts of the work of Jesus Christ, we must consider the subjective concepts of His work. These are the features of His work that take place within the person who receives Him by faith.

The Vital Concept. Within the discussion of the thanatological concept it was noted that death was a consequence of man's sin before God. As man, Christ took those death consequences on behalf of all mankind. Accepting that substitutional death of Jesus Christ, the Christian identifies with such as the death of the old man identity (Rom. 6:6), allowing him to be "dead to sin" (Rom. 6:2,11), to the world (Col. 2:20), to Law (Rom. 7:3,4; Gal. 2:19) and to the flesh (Gal. 5:24). We referred to this as the subjective aspect of the thanatological concept.

The Christian "passes out of death and into life" (John 5:24; I John 3:14), so we must proceed to consider the ontological reality of Christ's indwelling life in the Christian, which is just as surely the work of Christ as was the historical and objective work accomplished in His death. "Christ Jesus abolished death, and brought life and immortality to light through the gospel" (II Tim. 1:10), "granting us everything pertaining to life and godliness" (II Pet. 1:3).

Jesus is "the life" (John 14:6). "He that has the Son has life; he that does not have the Son of God does not have life" (I John 5:12). Jesus explained that He "came that we might have life, and have it more abundantly" (John 10:10). The "eternal life" (John 5:24) that activates us is His life. "Christ is our life" (Col. 3:4). "The life of Jesus is manifested in our mortal bodies" (II Cor. 4:10,11). We are "saved by His life" (Rom. 5:10) and "reign in life through Jesus Christ" (Rom. 5:17).

The theological term that is used to explain the vital concept of Christ's work is the word "regeneration." The word is used in the translation of Titus 3:5 referring to "the washing of regeneration and the renewal of the Holy Spirit." Regeneration implies being re-lifed, in conjunction with which the Bible uses the image of being "born again," "born from above," or "born of the Spirit" as Jesus explained to Nicodemus (John 3:1-6). Peter explains that we are "born again to a living hope through the resurrection of Jesus Christ from the dead" (I Peter 1:3), for it was in the resurrection of Jesus Christ that His life came forth out of death. Christians identify spiritually with the resurrection of Jesus, being raised "to newness of life" (Rom. 6:4).

The Spiritual Concept. In discussing the subjective concepts of Christ's work, it is extremely important to differentiate between subjective psychological effects within the Christian and the internal spiritual realities that Christ enacts by His own ontological presence. "If any man does not have the Spirit of Christ, he is none of His" (Rom. 8:9). The unregenerate person is spiritually dead, and can only be made spiritually alive by the presence of the Spirit of Christ for "it is the Spirit who gives life" (John 6:63; II Cor. 3:6). "That which is born of the Spirit is spirit" (John 3:6).

A spiritual exchange takes place in our spirit when Christ begins to work within us. Instead of "the spirit of slavery," we have the "spirit of adoption" (Rom. 8:15). We no longer have "the spirit from the world," but we have the "Spirit of God" (I Cor. 2:12). The "spirit of error" is exchanged for the "spirit of truth" (I John 4:6). The "spirit that works in the sons of disobedience" (Eph. 2:2) is replaced by the "Spirit of Christ" (Rom. 8:9; Phil. 1:19), the "Spirit of God" (I Cor. 3:16), "the Holy Spirit who dwells in us" (II Tim. 1:14). We are no longer "by nature children of wrath" (Eph. 2:3), but we become "partakers of the divine nature" (II Peter 1:4).

"Joined to the Lord, we are one spirit with Him" (I Cor. 6:17), for the "Spirit of holiness is Jesus Christ our Lord" (Rom. 1:4); "the Lord is the Spirit" (II Cor. 3:17). "We have become partakers of Christ" (Heb. 3:14). Christ lives in us

(Gal. 2:20), the "hope of glory" (Col. 1:27), "dwelling in our hearts through faith" (Eph. 3:17). "Do you not recognize that Jesus Christ is in you?" (II Cor. 13:5).

The Functional Concept. The internal work of Jesus Christ in the Christian is for the purpose of expressing a functional humanity wherein "the life of Jesus is manifested in our mortal bodies" (II Cor. 4:10,11). In like manner as Jesus indicated that "the Father abiding in Me does His works" (John 14:10), the Christian is to function by allowing the indwelling Christ to work through him. "Apart from Me, you can do nothing" (John 15:5), Jesus said. Paul explained that he did "not presume to speak of anything, except what Christ had accomplished through him" (Rom. 15:18).

Several theological terms have been traditionally defined by objectified reference to the historical work of Jesus Christ. As such they become static concepts which fail to do justice to the functional work of Jesus Christ in the Christian. "Salvation," for example, is not just the "threshold factor" of the Christian life whereby one is "made safe from going to hell." Rather, salvation must be viewed as the dynamic ontological function of the Savior, wherein we are being "saved by His life" (Rom. 5:10). The Christian is "made safe" from dysfunctional humanity, the misuse and abuse of Satan, in order to function as God intended by the indwelling presence and activity of the risen Lord Jesus in his behavior. Likewise, "sanctification" is the functional expression of God's character of holiness in the behavior of man.

The Relational Concept. Due to sin, man's relationship with God was disconnected. Man was "without God in the world" (Eph. 2:12), and "excluded from the life of God" (Eph. 4:18). There was an "enmity" (Eph. 2:15,16) between

95

God and man, to the extent that man was viewed as an "enemy" of God (Rom. 5:10). Fallen man was "alienated" (Col. 1:21) and "hostile toward God" (Rom. 8:7).

The work of Jesus Christ effects a "reconciliation" between God and man that can be viewed both objectively and subjectively. "God was in Christ reconciling the world to Himself" (II Cor. 5:19,20). "He reconciled all things to Himself, having made peace through the blood of His cross" (Col. 1:20). "We were reconciled to God through the death of His Son, and having been reconciled we are now saved by His life" (Rom. 5:10).

The Christian has a personal relationship with God. The reconciled relationship that we now have with God through Jesus Christ is such that we can view it as the social and familial relationship of being "adopted as sons through Jesus Christ" (Gal. 4:5; Eph. 1:5), and can cry out in the familiarity of the child's cry of "Abba, Father" (Rom. 8:15).

The Ontological Concept. The work of Jesus Christ is always ontological. He does what He does, because He is who He is! All that is made available to us in Jesus Christ is ontologically connected with His Being. He did not come to bestow various spiritual "benefits" upon mankind, but He came that His very Being might become functionally operative in mankind.

The saving activity of Jesus Christ is only operative when the Being of the Savior is at work in the Christian. Salvation cannot be ontologically divorced from the Savior. The process of sanctification is taking place only when the ontological expression of the Being of God's holy character is being manifested in man's behavior.

Perhaps the greatest perversion of Christian terminology has been to restrict the meaning of "justification" to an objectified declaration of pardon, acquittal, forgiveness and "right standing" with God. "Justification" is the word for righteousness. Righteousness is not merely a legal term, but explains the ontological character of God. God is righteous! (Ps. 116:5; Isa. 45:21; Dan. 9:14; Rom. 1:7). Jesus is referred to as "the Righteous One" (Acts 3:14; 7:52; 22:14), and "Jesus Christ, the Righteous" (I John 2:1). "God made Him who knew no sin, to be sin on our behalf, that we might become the righteousness of God in Him" (II Cor. 5:21). By the indwelling presence of Jesus Christ, He has "become to us righteousness" (I Cor. 1:30), "a righteousness that comes from God on the basis of faith" (Phil. 3:9). We have "the gift of righteousness in order to reign in life through Jesus Christ" (Rom. 5:17). The work of Christ continues as He ontologically expresses His character of righteousness in Christian behavior.

In addition to the objective and subjective concepts of Christ's work noted above, all of which have solid biblical notation, there are some other concepts which have been suggested which seem to be invalid because they lack biblical support. Most of these concepts of the work of Christ posit humanistic concepts of human potential whereby man's performance and "works" affect the relationship between God and man. They fail to understand that man is spiritually derivative and contingent, designed to function by the ontological dynamic of the Being of God generating His character in man's behavior.

Hugo Grotius, a lawyer, (1583-1645) suggested a sub-concept of the legal and penal concept, which might be called the *governmental or political concept.* Based on somewhat dualistic premises, Grotius suggested that God had to keep his authoritative government intact, so the punitive consequences were to "preserve God's authority."

Much of Western theology has had a tendency to view the work of Christ in almost total objectivity, causing it to be limited to a belief-system. Christ's work is regarded as historical or theological data that Christians must assent to the veracity of, thus becoming but a *doctrinal, theological or epistemo - logical concept.*

On the opposite end of the spectrum is the *mythical con - cept* suggested by Rudolph Bultmann (1884-1976). Historicity is regarded as irrelevant, and the work of Christ becomes totally subjective as the experiential impact it has on a person's life. The veracity of historical "myths" and "stories," even the death of Jesus Christ, might be questioned without affecting the subjective work of Christ.

The *mystical or symbolical concepts* of the work of Christ are also quite subjective. Images such as the "blood of Christ" and the "cross of Christ" are envisioned as entities in and of themselves which effect the work of Christ within the believer. Jesus Christ is regarded as working in the Christian when he is "appropriating the cross" or "applying the blood."

Socinius (1539-1604) suggested the *illustrational or imi - tational concept* of the work of Christ. He, along with others, emphasized that Jesus was an example of love, righteousness, obedience, dedication, commitment and sacrifice. Scripture does indicate that "Jesus suffered for us, leaving us an example to follow in His steps" (I Peter 2:21). Jesus did say, "If anyone would come after Me, let him deny himself, and take up his cross daily, and follow Me, willing to lose his life for My sake" (Luke 9:22-24). We are to "walk in the same manner as he walked" (I John 2:6), but the purpose of Christ's life and death is more than an example of self-denial and self-sacrifice of time, energy and reputation, even unto martyrdom. Such a concept fails to understand the ontological derivativeness of mankind.

Likewise, to project the work of Christ primarily as the ultimate teacher in an *instructional or educational concept,* fails to grasp man's spiritual contingency. Jesus was a teacher (Matt. 19:16; John 3:2), and did indicate that He came "to bear witness to the truth" (John 18:37), but He also explained that He was the Truth (John 14:6), ontologically embodied. Jesus did not come just to instruct us how to live and die, but He came to be the Truth of God lived out through man.

The *influential concept* of Christ's work was emphasized by Peter Abelard and later by Horace Bushnell. With an aversion to considering the wrath of God, the love of God was promoted as God's primary objective in what Christ did. "God so loved the world that He gave His only begotten Son" (John 3:16). "God demonstrated His love toward us, in that while we were yet sinners, Christ died for us" (Rom. 5:8). God's love is said to be for the purpose of influencing or motivating man to love in like manner. "We love, because He first loved us" (I John 4:19). When we respond to this divine influence, we are allegedly "saved" from the erroneous thinking of fear and shame, and the sickness of our sin is healed. In conjunction with the foregoing concepts, this concept fails to understand that man functions only by derivation, and that "the love of God has been poured out in our hearts by the Holy Spirit who was given to us" (Rom. 5:5), expressed only as a "fruit of the Spirit" (Gal. 5:22).

A most pervasive misconception of the work of Christ is the *ethical or moral concept.* Christ took upon Himself the "curse" of the Law (Gal. 3:13), and forgave our sinful violations of the Law, but now Christians are expected to continue to keep the Law in order to exhibit Christian behavior. Christian behavior is externalized into conformity with particular standards of what is "good" or "right." The work of Jesus is regarded as inciting the Christian to ethical and moral behavior, in order to be pleasing to God and to live the Christian life.

The concepts which have Biblical support are both objective and subjective. If the objective concepts are over-emphasized to the neglect of the subjective concepts, the objectification fails to do justice to the ontological dynamic of the life of the risen Lord Jesus. The work of Christ is cast into historical and theological categories which focus on the remedial action of Christ upon the cross, whereupon He took the death consequences for our sins. If the subjective concepts are over-emphasized to the neglect of the objective concepts, then the objective foundation of Jesus Christ is "mythified" or "mystified," leaving Christ's work to float in the breeze of subjective human thought. A balanced combination of objective and subjective concepts must be maintained. The remedial action of Christ's work on the cross must be understood in conjunction with the restorational action of Christ in the resurrection, ascension, Pentecostal outpouring, and continued intercessional work.

All of the concepts must be taken into account as we attempt to comprehend the work of Christ. The concepts, which are suggested by various images and identified with various terminology, still remain inadequate human representations of what Jesus Christ has done and is doing. Individually, or even collectively, they cannot encompass the whole of God's action on man's behalf. A balanced view of these concepts, with the recognition that all is effected only by ontological connection with, and derivation from, Jesus Christ, can lead us to as complete an understanding as is possible by the finite apprehension of man.

Models

Throughout the history of Christian thought the foregoing concepts have been developed into various models in order to systematize theological thought. Particular perspectives have been formed into logical mind-sets to create a paradigm of conceptualization. The composite mental construction with its unique postulates, data and inferences becomes a lens through which the work of Jesus Christ is viewed, and a pattern by which theology is promulgated.

Three particular models will be considered in this study, though these are not by any means exhaustive of all Christian thought through the ages. These mental constructs do not come complete with labels, so we will take the liberty to entitle them (1) the legal/penal model, (2) the personal/relational model, and (3) the spiritual/ontological model, the latter being proposed as an alternative to the other two which seem to have predominated throughout the history of Christian theological thought. (Consult chart on page 112.) All of these models can claim a Biblical base, employing Biblical documentable images which align with certain Biblical concepts. Our objective is to discover a model which provides the most comprehensive explanation of the totality of Christ's work.

The Legal/Penal Model obviously constructs its thinking primarily from the legal and penal concept of Christ's work, though several of the other concepts are integrated into such. This creates a model that is judicial and forensic in outlook.

God is viewed as the ultimate authority who issues decrees of His intent and expectations for man. There are precepts and standards, rules and requirements which explain what He expects. The Divine Lawgiver has codified His expectations in the Law, and His justice demands that He act

101

as Judge to ensure that His authority is respected and His expectations enacted.

There is an underlying presupposition in the legal/penal model that seems to accept the invalid ethical or moral concept. It seems to convey the idea that God intends for man to perform in accordance with the Law, to keep the Law by human "works."

Man's response to God's intent is a choice either to accept the sense of obligation and responsibility to do what God expects and keep the Law, or to choose to disobey and disregard what God desires, violating His Law.

The historical offense against God in Adam's sin is regarded as primarily a legal offense, a violation of the just demands and requirements of God's Law. The images of transgression, trespass, and a crime deserving of punishment are emphasized. Sin is defined as "missing the mark" of God's Law and His righteous expectations for man. "Sin is lawlessness" (I John 3:4). "All unrighteousness is sin" (I John 5:17). The sins of mankind are regarded as violations of God's standards.

Consequences are demanded by God for the violation of His Law. Punishment must be imposed and man must face judgment. Man is regarded as condemned and under a curse. Violation demands retribution, even the death penalty.

The required remedy for God's violated law is that the death penalty must be taken. There must be reparation, restitution, compensation. Only thereby can amends be made for violated Law. As man, Jesus could serve as the substitute who would take the penalty of death for sin and satisfy the just demands of the Law, allowing for pardon and commutation for the human race. The action of Jesus Christ on the cross allowed for "salvation," being made safe from the penalty of sin; "forgiveness," acquittal, the pardon of dismissed charges;

and "justification" whereby righteousness is credited to our account and we are "declared righteous." Redemption is effected as the "certificate of debt" (Col. 2:14) was taken to the cross by Jesus. The "ransom" has been paid.

The legal/penal model emphasizes the remedial aspects of Christ's work, and seems to be weak in its explanation of the restorational work of Christ. Man is free from the penalty of sin in everlasting death; free from going to hell, and free to go to heaven. The Christian is placed once again into an obligation of obedience which necessitates the keeping of the Law and the responsibility for moral and ethical behavior in accord with God's standards. Failure to keep the law requires the ascended Jesus to intercede for the Christian as a legal advocate (I John 2:1) before God, the Judge.

This model tends to be heavily weighted toward the objective concepts of Christ's work, and in particular focuses on the legal and penal concept to the neglect of others. It has probably been the predominant model throughout the whole of Christian history. Several of the early Christian writers and theologians were lawyers and couched their theological thinking in concepts of Roman law. The Protestant Reformation continued the legal/penal model by their emphasis on legal "justification."

The Personal/Relational Model has been presented in various forms throughout the history of Christian theology. It has often surfaced as a response against the legal/penal model, attempting to construct a model that is based on God as relational Person, rather than Judge.

God is viewed in social and psychological terms. The wrath of God and the love of God are emphasized. God loves man and has a plan for each person's life, desiring that each individual know and do His will. The intent of God was for man to remain in a relationship of personal fellowship, wherein man would submit to God's personal direction in his life.

The choice that man had before God was either to obey by maintaining the intended personal, social relationship of harmony and oneness with God, respecting God's personal authority as Lord and living in accord with His plan and His will, or man could disobey by failing to meet God's preferences and personally offend Him.

The offense of man against God is viewed primarily as a personal offense that causes a break in the relationship. Man has rebelled against a loving Lord. Sin is regarded as "missing the mark" of God's personal expectations, plans and pleasures. Behavioral sins are personal failures which personally wrong, slight and affront God.

God is personally upset by the broken relationship of unfulfilled expectations. He has been dishonored. His dignity has been offended. The wrath of God is emphasized as consequence of man's failure.

Man is alienated and separated from personal relationship with God. He is estranged from God, to the point of enmity and hostility that would cause him to be an enemy of God. God, on the other hand, demands to be satisfied, demanding payment, even death.

The only way that God can be appeased and pacified is for man to suffer His wrath in death. Jesus is the substitute on which God vents and expresses His personal wrath against man's sin of broken relationship. God is pleased and content with what Jesus does on man's behalf. His wrath is placated and mollified.

Based on the remedial action of Jesus Christ, God is willing to personally forgive man for his sin of rebellion. Man can experience "salvation," safe from estrangement with God.

A "personal relationship" is established with God through Jesus Christ, as man is "reconciled" with God. "Justification" is a right relationship that respects the rightful authority of God.

The personal/relational model is also primarily a remedial model, weak in its restorational emphasis. Man is free from estrangement and reconciled to God in personal fellowship, but is responsible for obedience which necessitates his being in a submitted relationship to God, living in accord with His plan and His will. The inevitable failures are resolved as the living Christ makes personal intercessory pleas on our behalf before God.

This model tends to be quite subjective as it emphasizes the relational and social concept of Christ's work. Anselm (1033-1109) and Peter Abelard (1079-1142) championed this model of atonement, and may have done so because the idea of "offended lords" fit better with the social milieu of feudalism that was the context in which they lived. Many others have suggested variations of this model since that time, especially in modern times with the increased emphasis on psychological and social relationships.

The Spiritual/Ontological Model is an attempt to explain the work of Christ in a way that gives adequate import to all of the Biblical concepts.

This model commences with a view of God that focuses on His character. The God who is Spirit (John 4:24) is absolutely perfect, holy, righteous, good and loving. God *does* what He *does* because He *is* who He *is*. All of His doing is derived from His Being. He created man as a dependent, contingent and derivative creature, that he might be receptive in faith to actively express the divine character in human behavior.

The choice of mankind was either to obey by "listening under God" to determine His direction and to derive His character expression, or to disobey by choosing not to depend on God in order to derive and receive from God.

The offense of man against God is viewed as a spiritual offense. The original disobedience and sin of man was a repudiation of the spiritual condition and behavioral expression that God intended. It was a rejection of the ontological indwelling of God in man, and therefore a rejection of the spiritual life, identity and nature of God. Man was in essence indicating that he did not want to be connected to the Being of God, dependent, contingent and receptive from God, for he was duped by the Deceiver with the lie that he could be autonomous, independent and self-generative.

Sin is defined as "missing the mark" of God's character, contradicting His character by failing to act out of the ontological energizing of Divine generation of character. Sinful behavior is the expression of the character of the Evil One, also ontologically derived from his spiritual being.

God has a passion for the preservation of His absolutely perfect character expression. Even the Law was given for the purpose of explaining His character. Contrariety of His character brings forth the wrath of God that is directed not so much against man, but against the satanic source of sin.

The consequences that came upon man because of sin were inherent within and demanded by the character of God. God is singularly absolute perfection. The unified perfection of His character cannot be contaminated, defiled, corrupted, adulterated, severed, broken or dissected. The Perfect cannot tolerate the imperfect. There can be no integration, merging or communion with that which is unholy. "God cannot deny Himself" (II Tim. 2:13), and cannot overlook that which is contrary to His character within His creation. Contrariety, inconsistency, incongruity, incompatibility with the character of God logically demands separation, disconnection and detachment. So when man sinned against God the consequence was not just the absence or deprivation of God's ontological presence in man, "devoid of the Spirit" (Jude 1:19), but the consequence necessitated the ontological alternative of spiritual derivation from the contrary satanic character.

Sinful mankind is viewed as dysfunctional humanity, misused and abused by the spiritual source of sin in Satan (I John 3:8). Energized by the diabolic spirit (Eph. 2:2), man derives his spiritual condition and behavioral expression from the character of the Evil One.

The death consequence is not so much a penalty that God vindictively imposes upon man because of sin, but is ontological identification with the "one having the power of death, that is the devil" (Heb. 2:14). The consequence of man's destruction is not to be viewed necessarily as the punitive imposition of God, as ontological connection with the Destroyer. The spiritual consequence of man's fall into sin is the spiritual and ontological connection with the spirit of Satan. Fallen man is caught in "the snare of the devil, having been held captive by him to do his will" (II Tim. 2:26).

To counteract and sever the ontological connection and spiritual identification of mankind with the spirit of the Evil One (I John 5:19), only God could act to triumph over Satan and liberate mankind. Only the sovereign omnipotence of God could conquer the satanic source of sin and death, but He could only do so in a man who could and would assume the death consequences of sin. God's Son, Jesus Christ, was the God-man who would fulfill the necessary conditions of carrying out the divine requirements which would satisfy all consistency with God's character.

Jesus Christ was "made to be sin" (II Cor. 5:21) in like manner as the human race was "made sinners" (Rom. 5:19), taking upon Himself as a man the ontological connection with Satan in spiritual death. From the cross He exclaimed, "My God, My God, why have You forsaken Me?" (Matt. 27:46). The One who is life (John 14:6) became our substitutional representative in taking all the categories of death consequences, including physical death, spiritual death and everlasting death. In assuming such He healed such, just as the early Christian theologians noted that "the unassumed is the unhealed." In experiencing the imputation of sin and death the sinless One severed the ontological identification of humanity with the satanic source of sin and death. He "abolished death" (II Tim. 1:10), and destroyed the works of the source of sin (I John 3:8). He was "the first-born from the dead" (Col. 1:18; Rev. 1:5), bringing life out of death, that "He might be the first-born among many brethren" (Rom. 8:29) who in ontological identification with Himself could experience His resurrection-life. When the ontological connection of mankind with Satan in sin and death is cut off, then the ontological communion of life in Jesus Christ is made available to mankind.

Hence we begin to understand what Jesus meant when He exclaimed from the cross, "It is finished!" (John 19:30), a declaration that is inclusive of all the conceptual factors of His work noted earlier. Jesus was proclaiming that "The mission is accomplished. The usurpation of mankind by Satan is brought to an end; the captives are set free (liberation). The just consequences have been served (legal); the penalty has been fulfilled (penal). The indebtedness has been paid in full (economical). The sacrifice has been made (sacrificial). Death has been abolished (thanatological). The stain of sin is cleansed (purificational). This is the new covenant in My blood (covenantal). It's done; God has won (triumphal). God is satisfied that all has been done in accord with His character (transactional)."

Also inherent in the "finished work" of Jesus Christ is the realization that the restoration of man has been inexorably set in motion. The remedial work of Christ on the cross was not the termination of God's working in Christ. God never ceases to function in accord with His character, and there must be the continued outworking of the "finished work" of Jesus Christ. When death is taken, then the alternative ontological connection of life will of necessity be evidenced (vital). The spiritual exchange of ontological dependency can take place (spiritual). Man can once again function in a reconciled relationship of communion with God that derives from His Being. God's activity of grace continues in the on-going action of the risen Lord Jesus, by the dynamic of His life, restoring the ontological spiritual union of God and man.

The spiritual/ontological model gives due emphasis to the restorative work of Jesus Christ. Going beyond the emphasis on the remedial work of Christ, the results of which are often cast in terms of benefits bestowed by Christ's work, this model recognizes the divine objective of the ontological Being of God in Christ restored to function in man.

Regeneration is understood to be the ontological indwelling of the life of Father, Son and Holy Spirit. The Christian has experienced a spiritual exchange "from Satan to God" (Acts 26:18), and the risen Lord Jesus Christ lives in the Christian (Col. 1:27; Gal. 2:20; II Cor. 13:5). We are free to be man as God intended man to be, free to allow God's character to be expressed in our behavior to the glory of God. Justification is recognized as the Christian's being "made righteous" (II Cor. 5:21) by the spiritual/ontological indwelling of the "Righteous One" (I John 2:1), in order to manifest His character of righteousness in our behavior. Sanctification is conjoined with justification, allowing man to function as intended by the manifestation of the Holy character of God in man. Salvation is the comprehensive term that indicates that we have been "made safe" from the dysfunctional misuse and abuse of Satan, in order to function as God intended, deity functioning within humanity, Christ within the Christian.

Our obedience is the continuous "listening under" (*hupak - ouo*) God in order to discern and derive the expression of His character. The "finished work" of Jesus Christ implies that we continue to live by the activity of God's grace received through faith. It includes the complete work of Jesus Christ, for us, in us, and through us. Worship becomes the continuous expression of the "worth-ship" of His character in our behavior.

The spiritual/ontological model attempts to maintain a balance of the objective and subjective concepts of Christ's work, with a recognition of both the remedial and restorative work of Jesus Christ. It is based upon the fact that man is a derivative and contingent creature who functions only and always in spiritual and ontological dependency, receiving from one spiritual source or the other, from God or Satan.

Early in the history of Christian theology the features of this model were evident, in the writing of Irenaeus (c. 130-200), for example. He emphasized the victory of Christ, the liberation of man from Satan's control, and the restoration of man to God's intent. But through the centuries there has been a recurring tendency to cast the work of Christ into a legal/penal model or a personal/relational model, both of which are easier to understand and can more readily accommodate the humanistic premises of man's alleged autonomy and human potential. The spiritual/ontological model requires the acceptance of man's ontological and spiritual derivativeness as a human creature.

The spiritual/ontological model appears to best represent the Biblical explanation of the essential character of God, and the interaction of God and man. The legal/penal model and the Biblical images employed therein can and should be used as an explanatory analogy, but not as the primary model. The strengths of the legal/penal model are the recognition of the authority, justice and judgment of God; the guilt and condemnation of man's sin; the payment of the penalty by Jesus Christ; and the acquittal and pardon of man's sin through Jesus Christ. Likewise, the personal/relational model and the images employed therein can and should be used as explanatory analogy, but not as the primary model. The strengths of the personal/relational model are the recognition of God's love, wrath and inter-relational Personhood; the estrangement and alienation of man from God because of sin; Christ's taking God's wrath for man; and the reconciliation of God and man in personal relationship. Both the legal/penal and personal/relational models are weak in the presentation of the restorative work of Jesus Christ, failing to emphasize the living dynamic of the risen Lord Jesus and His on-going work in the Christian today. They both tend to divorce the Christian life from the spiritual life and ontological presence of Jesus Christ, which explains the necessary importance of the spiritual/ontological model.

May we always remember that the Divine work of God in Jesus Christ is such a unique spiritual reality that the images and concepts and models that we employ to explain such will always fall short of full understanding. Christians are obliged to seek to understand the work of Christ as best they can, but they must learn to live with finite limitations of understanding, and praise God for His "unfathomable ways" (Rom. 11:33).

Models of the Atonement

	Legal/Penal	Personal/Relational	Spiritual/Ontological
View of God and His intent	• God viewed as Lawgiver • God intends man to keep the Law • Man's choice to obey or disobey Law	• God viewed as personal & psychological • God wants man to submit • Man's choice to submit or rebel	• God viewed in terms of His character • God intends man to derive His character • Man's choice to receive or reject God
Offense of man against God.	• Regarded as legal offense • Transgression, trespass, violation • Sin is "missing mark" of God's Law	• Regarded as personal offense • Rebellion, broken relationship • Sin is "missing mark" of God's personal expectations and plans	• Regarded as spiritual offense • Rejection of God's presence, empowering • Sin is "missing mark" of God's character expression
Consequence of man's offense.	• Punishment, penalty, judgment, condemnation • Sinner viewed as guilty violator	• Alienation, separation, broken relationship • Sinner viewed as estranged, hostile enemy	• Devoid of God's presence; energized by satanic spirit • Sinner viewed as misused, abused humanity
Remedy for man's offense against God	• Necessity to make amends for violated Law • Satisfy demands of Law • Price to be paid: death penalty • Jesus Christ takes death penalty as our substitute • Man is declared "right with God," pardoned, acquitted	• Necessity to appease, placate, pacify God • Satisfy God's personal favor • Price to be paid: suffering wrath of God • Jesus Christ is substitute for God to vent His wrath • Man is reconciled to God in personal relationship	• Necessity to sever man's spiritual identification with Satan • Satisfy consistency with God's character • Price to be paid: abolishment of death and its source • Jesus Christ is substitutional representative to take death consequences • Man is ontologically invested with spiritual life of God
Restoring man to God's intent.	• Free from penalty of Law • Christ intercedes as Advocate	• Free from estrangement with God • Christ intercedes with personal pleas before God on man's behalf	• Free to be man as God intended • Christ is our life as Christians

112

7

The Response of Man

The "finished work" (John 19:30) of God in the work of His Son, Jesus Christ, provides everything necessary for man to be restored to function as God intended. Can anything or anyone, other than God Himself, limit the application of the restorative work of God in Christ? To admit such would be to deny the unlimited power, the omnipotence of God, and posit the existence of a greater power than God who could limit the power of God. Though God "cannot deny Himself" (II Tim. 2:13) and limit Himself essentially, He can self-limit Himself functionally in order to function in a particular manner in conjunction with His creation, just as the divine Messiah did in "emptying Himself" (Phil. 2:7), in order to function in a particular way, as a man. This God has done by creating man as a choosing creature. God self-limited Himself functionally to act in correspondence with the choices that man might make to depend upon Him and derive from Him in a personal faith-love relationship. God did not create man with an absolute free-will, for such is the attribute and prerogative of God alone, but He did create mankind with a freedom of choice whereby he could choose to derive his spiritual condition and behavioral expression from one spiritual source or the other, God or Satan.

In his original created condition, Adam had the choice to accept or reject a relationship of contingency upon the Creator. With this choice of derivation he chose to derive from other than God, deceived by the Deceiver into thinking that he could be self-generative, "like God" (Gen. 3:5). The freedom of derivative choice, though, is part of human crea-tureliness. The derivative choosing capacity of man was not damaged, extracted or forfeited by the fall of man into sin. Man always functions by receiving the consequences of his choices (Col. 3:25). Fallen mankind is functioning by the consequence of his chosen contingency, but retains the humanness of being a choosing creature.

The Necessity of Man's Response

God's activity within the work of His Son, Jesus Christ, for the restoration of the human race, necessitates a response from man. Man is responsible, might we say response-able, to respond to God's action of grace in Jesus Christ. Derivative response-ability does not in any way imply the ability for self-generative activity which can work or perform or do any-thing that has any merit before God. Such would be contrary to man's human derivativeness. But as a human creature, man has the ability to respond derivatively to spiritual presence and activity. Whereas fallen man has been a "slave of sin" (John 8:34; Rom. 6:6) and "held captive by the devil to do his will" (II Tim. 2:26), the option for man to respond to God's ontological presence and activity has been made available by the remedial and restorative work of Jesus Christ, and it is necessary for man to respond to such either in derivative acceptance or rejection.

Two different systems of thought deny the necessity of man's response in derivative choice to God's activity of the restoration of man in Jesus Christ. These two extremist positions have errors that are similar, yet at the same time they are antithetical one to the other.

The first thesis is that man has no need to concern himself with responding to God's work in Jesus Christ, for God will see to it that all men will respond eventually. This view of the extent and efficacy of Christ's atonement might be labeled **"inevitable universalism."** The proponents of this position emphasize the scriptural statements that "Christ died for all." Jesus "died for *all*, therefore *all* died;...He died for *all*" (II Cor. 5:14,15). He "gave Himself a ransom for *all*" (I Tim. 2:6), to "bring salvation to *all* men" (Titus 2:11), resulting in "justification of life to *all* men" (Rom. 5:18). "By the grace of God Jesus tasted death for *everyone*" (Heb. 2:9), and is therefore "the propitiation for our sins, and for those of the *whole world*" (I John 2:2). "Does 'all' mean 'all'? Does 'everyone' mean 'everyone'?," questions the professor propagating this teaching. The first fallacy of thought lies in the all-inclusive categorization of "all" as representing all mankind, failing to recognize that "all" can be used restrictively in the sense of "all who respond." A second fallacy is in the failure to understand that Christ died for all mankind in terms of objective sufficiency, but such only becomes subjectively efficacious in all who respond with receptivity. James Moffatt notes that

> "when the grace of God is represented as an unconditioned boon or offer, the logical deduction is a salvation for all, irrespective of their personal acceptance,...an objective salvation without any subject element corresponding to it."[1]

The doctrine of "unconditional election" when pushed to its extreme often results in such a theological conclusion of "inevitable universalism." Advocating that *all* men will in one way or another at some time or another be restored to God, some indicate that men will even have a second chance after death when "the gospel is preached to those who are dead, that...they may live in the spirit according to the will of God" (I Peter 4:6).

The second error proposes that man has no need to concern himself with responding to God's work in Jesus Christ, for God will see to it that the chosen few who were predetermined in advance will respond as He sees fit in accord with His timing. This view of the extent and efficacy of Christ's atonement might be labeled the **"arbitrary limitation"** of man's response. Calvinistic theology refers to the "limited atonement" of Christ, indicating that God has predestined and elected certain individuals to participate in Christ's redemptive efficacy. Those individuals not thus elected cannot and will not respond. W. Ian Thomas remarks,

> "Some would have you believe that only those can obey the Gospel and accept Christ as their Saviour, to whom God has given the ability to obey as a purely arbitrary, mechanical act on His part, leaving no option in the matter to any individual either way! ...such an idea can only serve to bring the righteousness and judgment of God into contempt and disrepute. It is your inherent right to choose which is at the very heart of the mystery, both of the mystery of godliness and of the mystery of iniquity."[2]

> "Never allow anyone to deceive you into believing that God has placed an arbitrary limitation upon the efficacy of the blood of Christ, or that there are those who cannot repent, even if they would, simply because God has deliberately placed them outside the scope of His redemptive purpose! This blasphemes the grace, the love and the integrity of God, and makes Him morally responsible for the unbelief of the unbeliever, for the impenitence of the impenitent, and saddles Him squarely with the guilt of the guilty – as an

aider and abettor of their sin! Such is not the teaching of the Bible, for the Lord Jesus Christ made it abundantly clear that the reluctance is on man's part, not on God's! (Luke 13:34; John 3:19)"[3]

We must not dilute the love and grace of God and make Him responsible for the damnation of designated men. "God is not one to show partiality" (Acts 10:34). "God is not willing that any should perish, but that all should come to repentance" (II Peter 3:9). "God desires all men to be saved, and to come to the knowledge of the truth" (I Tim. 2:4).

The similarities in these two systems of thought is evident as they both commence with the thesis that their perceived intent of God's activity in Jesus Christ determines the extent of its application. The universalist believes that Jesus died for all men, and therefore all men will respond. The limitationist believes that Jesus died for particular individuals, and those particular individuals will respond. Both deny the responsibility of man to respond to God's action in Jesus Christ, for God is made responsible for the extent of human response that accords with His determined intent. Arbitrary determination of God's intent and inevitable application of the extent of man's response are indicative of both. The antitheses of these two concepts is in the extent of God's intent and divinely enacted response within those men thus determined. Is it universal or limited? The first is too broad, the second too narrow.

The "finished work" of Jesus Christ is objectively sufficient for all men. It becomes personally and subjectively efficacious for those men who respond in the receptivity of faith. There is the possibility and necessity of man's response to what God has made available in Jesus Christ. Those who exercise their freedom of choice in the receptivity of faith in Jesus Christ will derive their spiritual condition and behav-

117

ioral expression from the ontological presence and activity of the risen Lord Jesus in order to function as God intended.

A Solicited Response

God has taken the initiative to act on man's behalf through His Son Jesus Christ. "While we were yet sinners" (Rom. 5:8) and "enemies" (Rom. 5:10), "God demonstrated His love toward us." "God so loved the world that He gave His only begotten Son" (John 3:16). "When the kindness of God our Savior and His love for mankind appeared, He saved us" (Titus 3:4,5). "The grace of God appeared, bringing salvation to all men" (Titus 2:11).

God's activity was not terminated in the historical acts of the death, burial, resurrection and ascension of Jesus Christ. In accord with His character of love and grace, God continues to take the initiative to solicit man's response, knowing that such will serve the highest good of man in restoring him to the functional expression of divine character that God intended for man when He first created man. Such a solicitation of man's response does not imply a divine predeterminism that negates man's freedom of choice. The solicitation of the serpent in the garden of Eden did not impinge upon man's freedom of choice, and neither does the solicitation of the Spirit of God encouraging man to make a choice of dependency, contingency, derivation from God, and receptivity of Jesus Christ.

The objective sufficiency of Christ's work, which transpired historically almost two millennia ago, must be shown to relate to individuals in our age. The response of man is founded on objective reference; something happened, outside of ourselves, to which and to Whom mankind must relate in order to function as intended. That person was Jesus Christ;

the historical events included His death, resurrection, ascension and Pentecostal outpouring; and the theological implications include the remedial and restorative aspects of His work on man's behalf. Mankind is not asked to respond to questionable "mythical" or "mystical" phenomena in a purely subjective response which might produce an experiential feeling of well-being or peace, or as some allege, "a divine warmth," "an inner buzz," "warm fuzzies," or "a burning bosom." The legitimate subjective implications of Christ's work must be based on the historically objective work of Christ.

It is difficult for many contemporary men to understand and accept how the actions of another who lived long ago can affect their spiritual condition and life. Just as the action of Adam affected the human race by the establishment of spiritual solidarity with Satan, so the work of Jesus Christ can establish a spiritual solidarity with Himself for those who will respond in a choice of receptivity.

The solicitation for such a response was alluded to by Jesus when He spoke prophetically, prior to His death, that "when He was lifted up (in crucifixion, rather than ascension), He would draw all men to Himself" (John 12:32). This solicitory activity is done by the Spirit of Christ. Jesus explained to His disciples that He would need to depart in order that He might return again in Spirit-form (John 14:26; 15:26; 16:7). The promised Comforter, Intercessor and Solicitor would be "another" (John 14:16), like unto Himself, for it would indeed be He who came (John 14:18,28) in Spirit-form. Approximately forty days after the crucifixion of Jesus, He ascended to the Father, and ten days later returned on Pentecost in the form of the Holy Spirit to continue His ministry of drawing all men to Himself.

To expedite the process of soliciting man's response to the work of Jesus Christ, the Holy Spirit, utilizing the correspondence skills of finite men, inspired a written record of what God had done and wanted to do for man in Christ. "All Scripture is inspired by God" (II Tim. 3:16), and serves as the tangible, objective standard by which men can know and determine the historical and theological veracity of God's activity.

Herein we begin to discover the instrumentality of God's solicitation of man's response; the agent and the means which are employed to solicit a response in man. The Holy Spirit poured out on Pentecost utilizes the scriptures He inspired and the proclamation of Spirit-filled individuals to evoke a response in man. The Spirit of God is the active and personal agent. The proclamation of the gospel, whether by written, verbal or behavioral expression, constitutes the general means. Paul explains this instrumentality to the Thessalonians when he wrote, "our gospel did not come to you in word only, but also in power and in the Holy Spirit and with full conviction; You received the word in much tribulation with the joy of the Holy Spirit" (I Thess. 1:5,6).

Caution must be advised about limiting the phrase "word of God" only to the written scriptures. The Spirit of Christ must not be limited to utilizing the written record of scripture exclusively, lest how can the gospel be proclaimed to the illiterate? Jesus is the eternal, living "Word of God" (John 1:1), the expression of God to man. His Spirit uses various proclamatory means; the ministry of men and of angels, providential circumstances, and every available medium of expression, to make known the gospel message of the "word of truth" (II Tim. 2:15), the "living and abiding word of God" (I Peter 1:23), the message of His Person and His work. This is done in consistency with the objective record of the Spirit-inspired scriptures, and not in contradiction thereto.

There have been some who have so emphasized the biblical means of God's solicitation of man's response, that they have denied the active and personal agency of the Holy Spirit. This seems to have been a constant temptation throughout the history of the Church. Tertullian (160-230 A.D.) once lamented that "the Holy Spirit has been chased into a book." Roman Catholic theologians objected to the Protestants ascribing so much authority to the Bible in their doctrines of *sola scriptura,* that they had effectively "imprisoned God in a book" and constructed a "paper pope." We must beware of a biblicism that becomes bibliolatry, remembering that Christianity is not a book-religion, but is the dynamic revelation of God in Jesus Christ. The Holy Spirit must not be relegated to but an illuminative influence that comes through reading the Bible, but must be recognized as the active and personal agency of Jesus Christ Himself in drawing all men to Himself.

God takes the initiative in soliciting man's response to the work of Christ, and employs the instrumentality of the agency of the Holy Spirit and the means of proclamation, in order to exert a divine influence upon man urging and prompting him to respond without violating his freedom of choice. It is this soliciting influence of God that will now be considered.

The initial influence of God is that whereby God causes an individual to hear or otherwise be presented and confronted with the gospel of Jesus Christ. "Faith comes by hearing, and hearing by the word of Christ" (Rom. 10:17). "Did you receive the Spirit by the words of the Law, or by hearing with faith?" (Gal. 3:2). Such references to "hearing" must not be limited to audible sounds, for the deaf person also "hears" the presentation of the gospel. The setting for this "hearing" is providentially initiated and provided by God. Such is the providential right of God's influence. An individual may be directed to the right place and the right time to hear the right man with the right message. Looking back at such a situation an individual may exclaim that he does not know why he was there, but the situation provided him with the opportunity to hear of Christ's work.

God's influence also extends into the psychological realm of man's soul-function. Paul explains that "a natural man does not accept the things of the Spirit of God, for...he cannot understand them, because they are spiritually appraised" (I Cor. 2:14). It is necessary, therefore, that the Holy Spirit transcend our natural capabilities in order to influence mind and emotion. The good news of God's action in Jesus Christ is not perceived by human intellect or emotion, regardless of how such might be enhanced by higher education or by sensitivity training. The natural man in his fallen state needs some truths revealed to him, some illuminative revelation, some spiritual comprehension, some divine pricking of his conscience. The revelatory activity of God's Spirit is providentially "caught," not "taught." The teacher may teach, and the preacher may preach accurately and repeatedly, but by spiritual revelation "the light goes on," and an individual exclaims, "Oh, I see what God has done!" This is why this divine influence is referred to as being "enlightened" (Eph. 1:18; Heb. 6:4; 10:32) by a "revelation" (Eph. 1:17; Phil. 3:15) from God.

This provision of God's influence was promised by Jesus when He told His disciples, "I will send the Helper to you. And when He comes, He will convince (or convict) the world concerning sin, and righteousness, and judgment; concerning sin, because they do not believe in Me; and concerning righteousness, because I go to the Father, and you no longer behold Me; and concerning judgment, because the ruler of this world has been judged" (John 16:7-11). The Holy Spirit convinces and convicts in the mind and emotion of man. The original word *elengcho* in John 16:8 means "to bring to light" or "to expose," and that to whichever capacity it relates, whether mind or emotion.

The Holy Spirit seeks to convince the mind of the natural man that he is a "sinner" due to Adam (Rom. 5:19); that he is spiritually dead in trespasses and sins (Eph. 2:1,5); that Jesus was the perfect man, the God-man, who "died for our sins" (I Cor. 15:3) in order to give us His life (I John 5:12); that Satan was judged by the sacrifice of Christ and need not indwell us or control us (I John 3:8; Heb. 2:14); that we need not face judgment alone because Christ is our substitute (Rom. 8:1); that unbelief in Jesus Christ is unpardonable (Rev. 21:8); etc. The objective and subjective data of Christ's work can be presented to the mind of man for his "convincing," but this is more than an intellectual, academic or cerebral persuasion.

A similar process is enacted in the emotions of man by the convicting influence of the Holy Spirit. In exposing divine realities to our emotions we are convicted of sin which is contradictory to the character of God (Rom. 3:23); of our unrighteousness (Rom. 1:18; I John 1:9); of the judgment that will needlessly be incurred if we do not receive the substitutionary work of Jesus Christ (Rom. 6:23); etc. Such "conviction" can be an agonizing experience for the natural man, bringing forth fear, frustration of inadequacy and desperation. Isaiah cried out, "Woe is me, for I am ruined!" (Isa. 6:5). The crowd on Pentecost queried, "What must we do?" (Acts 2:37), and were ready to respond to God's activity in Jesus Christ.

Remember that God has self-limited Himself to operate in conjunction with man's responses. He will not violate or interfere with the volitional freedom of choice that He has granted to man by creation. God desires a voluntary response whereby man will receive Jesus Christ. He solicits such through the influence of man's mind and emotions, but He does not coerce man to consent with the will. Such would forestall a genuine faith-love relationship, for love cannot be coerced. Those who proclaim the gospel should likewise respect the choice of man and not attempt to force decisions through psychologically manipulated invitations and evangelistic methods, for such can develop hardened hearts in a pattern of resistance to the gospel.

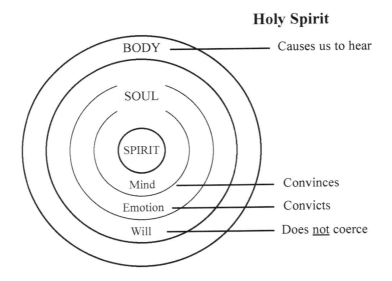

Holy Spirit

BODY — Causes us to hear

SOUL

SPIRIT

Mind — Convinces

Emotion — Convicts

Will — Does <u>not</u> coerce

A Comprehensive Response

A gift does not fulfill its purpose until it is received. Such receiving does not constitute any performance or "works" of human effort, but is simply the response of man to receive God's gracious restoration of man in Jesus Christ. God's autonomous, independent and self-generating activity of grace in Jesus Christ is intended to be received by a response of faith that dependently and contingently receives the very life of Jesus Christ in order to derive all from Him. "For by grace you have been saved through faith; and that not of yourselves, it is the gift of God; not as a result of works, that no one should boast" (Eph. 2:8,9).

Such a receptive response will of necessity involve the whole man and the totality of his function in spirit and soul and body. Man's response of faith must not be considered only as a spiritual, rational, experiential, volitional or activistic response. Faith does involve spiritual receptivity; mental assent and belief; the affections of trust, assurance and reliance; a choice of decision in the will; and the bodily confession of obedience, but no one level of response can be used to define the whole. Lewis Smedes refers to "the imperative of faith, and the urgency of accepting grace and responding to it in the totality of one's life"[4] We shall proceed to consider the comprehensive response of man to the work of Jesus Christ.

The spirit of man has no inherent capability of function. Some have speculated that fallen man has a "God-shaped vacuum" that creates an intrinsic "spiritual desire" to be indwelt by the Spirit of God. Biblical evidence is lacking for such a thesis. The spirit of man functions only as a receptacle of spiritual presence and activity. As the satanic "spirit is working in the sons of disobedience" (Eph. 2:2), the natural descendants of Adam, there is no desire or impetus therein to receive Jesus Christ. They are "alienated and hostile in mind" (Col. 1:21) toward God.

Man's Mind Responds

In response to the convincing solicitation of the Holy Spirit, the mind of man can respond in belief. "Whoever believes in Him shall not perish, but have eternal life" (John 3:16). "Believe in the Lord Jesus Christ, and you shall be saved" (Acts 16:31). "The gospel is the power of God unto salvation for everyone who believes" (Rom. 1:16). In the Greek language in which the New Testament was written, there is no differentiation made between "belief" and "faith." The same Greek word, *pistis,* is used for both concepts. In the mind of man there must be some degree of cognitive recognition and acceptance of the truth of the data about Jesus Christ. Though such a cognitive concurrence is necessary to the response of man, such belief cannot comprise the whole of man's response. James indicates that "the demons believe, and shudder" (James 2:19), but such does not comprise faith. Christianity is not only, or primarily, a belief-system wherein we give mental assent to the historicity of Jesus of Nazareth, or simply admit to the veracity of the Christian theological message. Over and over again throughout its history, the church has fallen prey to the "easy believism" which allows superficial acceptance of doctrinal data, and fails to explain the ontological receptivity of faith wherein we receive the very Being and life of Jesus Christ. Believing in the mind is necessary, but it is not the whole of faith.

Man's Emotions Respond

In response to the convicting solicitation of the Holy spirit, the emotions of man are intended to respond in godly sorrow. The conviction of sin, righteousness and judgment leads to an emotional brokenness, a consciousness of our helpless-

126

ness and hopelessness, a desperate awareness of inadequacy that compels a person to cry out, "God be merciful to me a sinner" (Luke 18:13). This is a much deeper response that just being "sorry" or having regret for our past sins. Godly sorrow is a genuine abhorrence and loathing of sin, the grief of contrition concerning the entire satanic pattern of evil, seeing such as heinous in the sight of God for it caused Jesus to be sent to the cross, and recognizing that we have been a willful slave of satanic activity (II Tim. 2:26) in direct contrast to God's intent. Like the Philippian jailer, we ask, "What must I do to be saved?" (Acts 16:30).

Man's Will Responds

The response of godly sorrow leads necessarily to the response of repentance, which involves both mind and will. "The sorrow that is according to God produces a repentance without regret, unto salvation" (II Cor. 7:10). The predominant Greek word for "repentance," and the word used in II Cor 7:10, is *metanoia,* which has to do with a changed mind that leads to a change of action. In repentance man is making a reasoned volitional response, a decision to allow the change of mind to effect a complete transformation of being and activity. The importance of this decision of repentance in the response of man to Christ is evident in the abundance of Scripture references to such. Jesus said, "I have come to call sinners to repentance" (Luke 5:32). Paul exhorted the Athenians, "God is now declaring to men that all everywhere should repent" (Acts 17:30), and explained to the Ephesian elders that he was declaring to everyone "repentance toward God and faith in our Lord Jesus Christ" (Acts 20:21). Peter indicates that "the Lord is not willing that any should perish, but that all should come to repentance" (II Peter 3:9). To the

127

Romans Paul wrote that "the kindness of God leads you to repentance" (Rom. 2:4). Having created men as choosing creatures, the volitional response in the will, wherein man chooses and makes a decision to accept and receive Jesus Christ and allow His derived life to make a change in behavioral expression is a key ingredient to man's response of faith.

Man's response of faith is more than just a psychological response though. Faith entails the comprehensive receptivity of God's activity. William Barclay noted that "the first element in faith is what we can only call receptivity," and that "not simply the receptivity of facts,"[5] but the receptivity of the person of Jesus Christ. John Calvin defined faith as "receiving what we need from Christ,"[6] and James Moffatt explained that faith is "the attitude of receptivity towards the gift of God."[7] W. Ian Thomas adds, "Faith involves that total dependence upon God which produces divine action in man."[8] The New Testament Scriptures likewise identify faith as receptivity, for John writes that "as many as received Him, to them He gave the right to become children of God, even to those who believe in His name" (John 1:12). Paul asks the Galatians, "Did you receive the Spirit by the works of the Law, or by hearing with faith?" (Gal. 3:2). To the Colossians he admonishes, "As you received Christ Jesus the Lord, so walk in Him...established in your faith" (Col. 2:6,7).

Faith is the determination to receive the ontological reality of God's Being and activity in Jesus Christ. It is not just the ideological option of believing certain evidence or data in order to make a logical decision, but encompasses the entire receptivity of the work of Christ. This includes the spiritual receptivity of the Spirit of Christ into the spirit of the man (Rom. 8:9), whereby the "spirit that works in the sons of disobedience" (Eph. 2:2) is displaced by "the Spirit who is from God" (I Cor. 2:12). It is the receptivity of a spiritual exchange whereby we are converted from "the dominion of Satan to God" (Acts 26:18). On the basis of the receptivity of man's faith response, the personal and subjective efficacy of Christ's work for us and in us takes place. The vital, spiritual, functional, relational and ontological implications of Christ's "finished work" become effective and operational with the receptive Christian.

There are certain Calvinistic theologians who would argue that faith is not the volitionally receptive response of man exercising his created freedom of choice to respond to the work of Christ, but is instead a response enabled and enacted by the activity of God. Misinterpreting texts concerning the "faith of the Son of God" (*KJV*-Gal. 2:20) and faith as "the gift of God" (Eph. 2:8), they allege that faith is not man's freely chosen response, but is elicited and enacted by God in man. More astute minds within the Calvinistic camp have denied that faith is God's act instead of man's. G.C. Berkouwer has written that "to ascribe faith to the grace of God is to invite subtle heresy."[9] John Murray states that "faith is not the act of God. Faith is a response on the part of the person and of him alone."[10] Writing the article on "faith" in *The Dictionary of New Testament Theology,* Rudolph Bultmann notes that "unlike Augustine, Paul never describes faith as a gift of God."[11]

The Augustinian/Calvinistic theology advocates the "arbitrary limitation" of Christ's work that was noted earlier, and denigrates the responsibility of man. Those individuals whom God has particularly predetermined to include within the extent of His saving work are unconditionally and spontaneously regenerated with the life of God, thereby empowering them to make a faith-response as a gift of God. This is not consistent with those Scriptures which indicate that the regenerative indwelling and activity of the Holy Spirit occurs when there is a freely chosen penitent response of faith in man's soul. "Having believed, you were sealed in Him with the Holy Spirit of promise" (Eph. 1:13). "As many as received Him, to them He gave the right to become children of God, to those who believe in His name" (John 1:12). "Believing you may have life in His name" (John 20:31).

It is important to reiterate that man's response of faith is not a performance of a "work" of human effort, to which God is obliged to respond in regenerating activity or any other activity. Faith does not "do" anything; it does not generate activity. The "doing" is done by the grace activity of God, who alone is self-generative. Faith is man's receptivity of God's activity; man's availability to God's ability; or as W. Ian Thomas says, "man's disposition that invokes God's Deity."[12] Does faith "move mountains"? (Matt. 17:20; I Cor. 13:2). Faith allows the power of God to move mountains!

Faith is not a condition or stipulation of human response which makes God's action contingent on man's response in a logical cause and effect relation. God has already taken the initiative to act on man's behalf in the "finished work" of Jesus Christ, and now solicits man's comprehensive response in a determinative choice of personal contingency upon Himself. Faith is man's choice to derive from God, depend upon God, and be receptive of God's activity, whether it be the remedial redemptive activity of God in Christ or the continuous restorative activity of God whereby He ontologically functions within the Christian.

Physical Manifestations of Faith Response

We proceed then to consider the manifestations of faith-response that are intended to occur within the body of man.

The body is the vehicle of expression, indicating that which transpires internally within the function of spirit and soul.

The responses of the body can all be categorized as "confession." Jesus said, "Everyone who shall confess Me before men, I will also confess him before My Father who is in heaven" (Matt. 10:32). The Greek word for confession is *homologeo*. It means "to say the same thing as," "to concur," "to agree." The actions of the body express agreement and concurrence with that which has taken place internally. The physical responses are the "follow-through" whereby the Christian indicates that he is "not ashamed of the gospel" (Rom. 1:16), and is willing to "let the redeemed of the Lord say so" (Psalm 107:2).

Verbal Confession

The first form of physical confession is verbal confession. Paul wrote to the Romans saying, "If you confess with your mouth Jesus as Lord and believe in your heart that God raised Him from the dead, you shall be saved; for with the heart man believes, resulting in righteousness, and with the mouth he confesses, resulting in salvation" (Rom. 10:9,10). John wrote similarly, "Whoever confesses that Jesus is the Son of God, God abides in him and he in God" (I John 4:15). The verbal confession is not causal for salvation or for the indwelling of God, but is evidentiary of such. By verbal agreement man makes known the inner subjective appropriation of Christ's function. This is obviously more than just mouthing a certain formula of words, whether the confession of Peter, "You are the Christ, the Son of the Living God" (Matt. 16:16), or some other prepared confession or creed. It is possible to profess and not possess. Jesus explained that some will come to Him, saying, "Lord, Lord," and He will respond by saying, "I do not know you" (Matt. 7:22,23; 25:11,12). There are some who verbally confess belief in Jesus, but Jesus does "not entrust Himself to them, for He knows all men" (John 2:24). Verbal profession alone is not sufficient; there must be verbal confession which agrees with the internal receptivity of God's activity in Jesus Christ.

Baptismal Confession

Another form of physical confession expresses the overt act of identification and agreement that God has always asked of His people. In the old covenant it was the physical circumcision of the males, whereas in the new covenant it is the act of baptismal confession. Again, the activity of the body must reflect what has transpired internally. The Christian explanation of baptism has always been that it is "an outward sign of an inward reality." A person is not "born again" in water baptism, as some would indicate in their theology of "baptismal regeneration." For the baptismal confession to be at all valid and legitimate it must be preceded by that which it signifies or symbolizes. Christian baptism in water is a public testimony or confession that this individual's spirit has been overwhelmed by the Spirit of God (Rom. 8:9,16), and this is being illustrated as the water overwhelms the body of this faithfully available person. The public action of baptism in water often becomes the overt act of public identification by which the Christian expresses agreement and concurrence with the reality of Christ's life in him forming the basis of his new identity in Christ.

132

Lifestyle Confession

A third form of confession in the body is the behavioral lifestyle that expresses agreement with the indwelling life and character of Jesus Christ. The supernatural life that we have received in Jesus Christ (John 14:6; I John 5:12) is to be supernaturally lived out in our behavioral expression. "It is no longer I who lives, but Christ lives in me" (Gal. 2:20). "Christ is our life" (Col. 3:4). This must be the ontological expression of "the life of Jesus manifested in our mortal bodies" (II Cor. 4:10,11), as man allows for the receptivity of His activity in faith. Paul advised the Colossian Christians, saying, "As you have received Christ Jesus the Lord, so walk in Him. . .established in your faith" (Col. 2:6,7). Christians have initially received Jesus Christ by the receptivity of His remedial and restorative activity in faith. They are to "walk" and live in Christ by the continued receptivity of His activity, the faith response for behavioral expression. "We are His workmanship, created in Christ Jesus unto good works which He has prepared beforehand, that we should walk in them" (Eph. 2:10). James postulates that the absence of such a consequential out-working of the activity of the life and character of Christ in a Christian's behavior is indicative of the absence of faith, properly defined. "Faith without works is dead" (James 2:17,26).

The comprehensive response of man to the work of Jesus Christ necessitates these various forms of physical confession and agreement. The receipt of Christ's presence and activity within must necessarily be antecedent to, not subsequent to, the responses of the body, though. Otherwise what is the mouth agreeing to? What does the baptism signify or symbolize? What dynamic means would we have for living a consistent Christian lifestyle that corresponds with the character of

Christ? Though it may be possible to have a counterfeit verbal confession and a counterfeit baptismal confession, it will be impossible to sustain a counterfeit lifestyle confession for any length of time. Jesus said, "By their fruit you shall know them" (Matt 7:16,20; 12:33). In the long term it is impossible to counterfeit "the fruit of the Spirit, which is love, joy, peace, patience, kindness, goodness, faithfulness, gentleness and self-control" (Gal. 5:22,23). These must be derived ontologically from the character of Christ within the Christian, by the faithful receptivity of His activity.

Mankind is always responsible for the response of faith. There is the initial receptivity of God's activity in the remedial and restorative activity of Jesus Christ; what some call "saving faith." There is the continual necessity of the "obedience of faith" (Rom. 1:5; 16:26) within the Christian life, as we continue to be receptive to the activity of Christ's work in our lives.

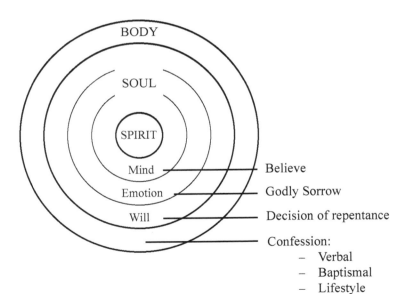

8

The Regeneration of Man

By the initiative of His grace through His Son Jesus Christ, God has accomplished everything necessary to restore mankind to the functional intent for which He created him. That divine intent was that His life and character might be present within the man, allowing for the expression of such in man's behavior unto the glory of God. Originally the spiritual life of God had been breathed into man (Gen. 2:7), but that divine life had been displaced by spiritual death, the personal resource of "the one having the power of death, that is the devil" (Heb. 2:14), when man willfully chose to respond to the satanic temptation in sin. Since all men were "in Adam" (I Cor. 15:22) and all the descendants of Adam come into being spiritually "dead in trespasses and sins" (Eph. 2:1,5), the need of mankind is to be "brought into being again" with the reinvestiture of divine life within man. This is the meaning of the term "regeneration": the prefix *re* is from the Latin language meaning "again"; generation is etymologically derived from the Latin *generare*, and that from the Greek *genesis*, which means "to bring into being" either by creation or by birth. This latter Greek word is the one affixed as a title to the first book of the Bible, *Genesis*, which obviously is the account of all things being "brought into being."

The Reason for Regeneration

Mankind did not need a new system of rehabilitation or reformation to deal with his sinful ways and the consequences of death. Additional rules and regulations to try to effect behavioral modification would not suffice. No amount of monies spent on public education in order to enhance and expand man's intellectual capabilities will ever solve man's spiritual problem. Least of all, will the man-made rituals, requirements and reforms of religion serve as any benefit for the resolution of man's problem, and the restoration of intended functionality.

Man's need is to be "brought into being again" spiritually. Perhaps we could say that man needs to be "re-genesized" in a similar manner as he was "genesized" in Genesis 2:7 when God breathed into man the Spirit of His own life and caused him to be spiritually alive by the presence of the divine life within the spirit of man. In his natural state due to the fall of man in sin, man is spiritually dead and needs to be spiritually revived.

Various metaphors are suggested by the regeneration concept of "bringing into being again." The term *genesis* has long been associated with creation, and the spiritual regeneration of man by the Spirit of Christ is illustrated as constituting the Christian as a "new creation" (II Cor. 5:17; cf. Gal. 6:15). Resurrection also pictures the concept of "bringing into being again," especially in portraying life out of death, and thus is used as a figure of regeneration when Christians are referred to as being "raised to newness of life" (Rom. 6:4). The predominant figure of regeneration is that of birth, of being "born again" with spiritual life. The Greek words associated with *genesis* are used over one hundred times in the New Testament in reference to birth, and this becomes the primary metaphor to explain regeneration. Jesus told Nicodemus that he needed to be "born from above," (John 3:3,7) to be "born of the Spirit" (John 3:5). Recent misuse of the terms "rebirth" or "born again" in some religious circles has caused the terms to be despised and caricatured by many today, but the image is indeed biblical.

The Resurrection Pre-requisite of Regeneration

The "finished work" (John 19:30) of Jesus Christ entails not only the objective remedial concepts of His work on the cross, but also the subjective restorative concepts of His work which derive from His resurrection, ascension and Pentecostal outpouring. The crucifixion of Jesus Christ alone would not have effected regeneration for all mankind. At the cross the remedial features were enacted when Jesus voluntarily and vicariously took the death consequences of man's sin upon Himself, but it was in the resurrection that life "came into being again" out of death, in order that such divine life could be made available to restore mankind. The negative death consequences for sin were taken care of at the cross, but the positive consequences of God's life made available to man were effected in the resurrection of Jesus. Biblical theology must always beware of focusing only on the cross of Christ without giving due emphasis to the resurrection. Christian theology was from its commencement a "resurrection theology." Peter's first sermon was that "God raised Him up again, putting an end to the agony of death" (Acts 2:24). Paul's proclamation was that "God had fulfilled His promises. . .in that He raised up Jesus" (Acts 13:33).

The resurrection of Jesus was the pre-requisite for regeneration. Using the illustration of a grain of wheat, Jesus explained that it had to die and come to life in order to bear much fruit (John 12:24). He was referring to His own death and resurrection, which would serve as the fruitful prototype of "many brethren" (Rom. 8:29) experiencing life out of death spiritually. "As Christ was raised from the dead, so we too might walk in newness of life, united in the likeness of His resurrection" (Rom. 6:4,5). Christians are "raised up with Christ" (Col. 2:12; 3:1), passing "out of death into life" (John 5:24; I John 3:14). Thus it is that Peter can declare that "God has caused us to be born again to a living hope through the resurrection of Jesus Christ from the dead" (I Peter 1:3), evidencing the pre-requisite of the historical resurrection of Jesus, with which we identify spiritually in regeneration.

Jesus explained to Martha, "I am the resurrection and the life; he who believes in Me shall live even if he dies" (John 11:25). The life of the risen Lord Jesus, the resurrection-life of Jesus, becomes the basis of spiritual life in the Christian.

The Reality of Regeneration

The essential reality of that which is "brought into being again" within the individual who receives Jesus Christ is not just a subjective experience of a "heart on fire" or a "peace within." Neither is it merely a judicial reality of "positional" right-standing with God, duly recorded as "justified" in the heavenly bookkeeping ledgers. Regeneration is not the receipt of a travel voucher, an eventual one-way ticket to heaven with the guarantee that one will not go to hell. The reality of regeneration is that the divine life of God is "brought into being again" within the spirit of the individual who receives Jesus Christ. The primary objective of Christianity is not how to get a man out of hell and into heaven, but to allow the life of God to be emplaced back into man that he might be functionally operative to the glory of God both on earth and in heaven.

There is only one way to get life. One cannot buy his way into life. Neither can one work his way into life. Being "made safe" from diabolic dysfunction, in order to function as God intended, never comes "on the basis of deeds which we have done in righteousness" (Titus 3:5), but only by regeneration. The only way to receive life is to be born into it, which evidences again the metaphor of "birth" as an illustration of regeneration. Being "born again" is not "turning over a new leaf" of religious dedication and commitment. It is not a renaissance of applied morality. It is the re-introduction of the divine life of Jesus Christ into the spirit of the individual who is receptive to such.

Regeneration encompasses the "vital concept" of Christ's "finished work" (cf. pg. 93). It is the restoration of the "personal resource of life" (cf. pg. 26), being the presence of the living God, reintroduced into the spiritual function capacity of man. Jesus said, "I came that you might have life, and have it more abundantly" (John 10:10). He identified this life which can be invested in us as the very essence of His own being, saying, "I am the way, the truth, and the life" (John 14:6). "He who has the Son has the life; he who does not have the Son of God does not have the life" (I John 5:12). Those who have been "made alive together with Christ" (Eph. 2:5), experience "Christ as their life" (Col. 3:4). It is a derived life that can never be separated from the being of Jesus Christ. As such it cannot be static. His life can never be viewed as a commodity to be possessed, an "eternal life package" which has value after our physical death. The reality of regeneration is that we receive the vital dynamic of the life of the risen Lord Jesus which is to have contemporary incarnational expression in the behavior of the Christian.

The Revelation of Regeneration

"The natural man does not accept the things of the Spirit of God; he cannot understand them, because they are spiritually appraised" (I Cor. 2:14). The fallen race of mankind does not naturally recognize their need for spiritual regeneration. "The god of this world has blinded the minds of the unbelieving, that they might not see the light of the gospel of the glory of Christ" (II Cor. 4:4). This is why Nicodemus, a religious "ruler of the Jews" (John 3:1), could not comprehend what Jesus was telling him when He explained, "You must be born again" (John 3:7); and "unless one is born again, he cannot see the kingdom of God" (John 3:3). Nicodemus was thoroughly religious, having attempted to keep all the Jewish moral regulations meticulously as a Pharisee (John 3:1), but he did not understand the spiritual implications of being "born again" and re-lifed with the indwelling presence of God's life. His spiritual ignorance was evidenced when he responded to Jesus, thinking only in terms of physical obstetrics, asking, "How can a man be born when he is old? He cannot enter a second time into his mother's womb and be born, can he?" (John 3:4). Jesus explained to Nicodemus quite simply that "unless one is born of water (physical birth) and the Spirit (spiritual birth), he cannot enter into the kingdom of God (wherein Christ reigns as Lord, as we reign in life through Him)" (John 3:5). Whether Nicodemus ever understood and was regenerated cannot be ascertained definitively, but he was sympathetic to Jesus and brought burial spices for the body of Jesus at His death (John 19:39).

In order to cause man to recognize the need for spiritual regeneration, the Spirit of God engages in the revelatory solicitation whereby Jesus "draws men to Himself" (John 12:32). It is not just a matter of religious education and catechism whereby one can intellectually perceive the need for such a spiritual exchange, but the revelation of such need and the availability of the provision of Jesus Christ, must be recognized in the enlightening and illuminating work of the Holy Spirit. Revelation is "caught," not "taught." God, in Christ, and by His Holy Spirit, solicits our response, working providentially even in the arrangement of circumstances whereby we are caused to hear the gospel. He convinces and convicts our mind and emotion "concerning sin, and righteousness and judgment" (John 16:7-11), thereby revealing our spiritual need and the provision for such need in Jesus Christ.

The Receipt of Regeneration

Regeneration becomes personally effectual for an individual when he is willing to receive the life of Jesus Christ in him by a freely chosen response of faith. "Belief" and "faith" are two English words which are both used to translate the Greek word *pistis*. Differentiation must be made, however, between a "belief" that is but mental assent to historical accuracy and theological orthodoxy, and the "faith" that is receptive to the spiritual life of Jesus Christ. Christianity is not just an epistemological belief-system of doctrinal data, despite the fact that religious perversions often project it to be such. One does not "believe in the Lord Jesus Christ" (Acts 16:31), in the same manner as one might believe that George Washington was the first president of the United States of America. Believing the veracity of the circumstantial historical data, one might assent and concur that George Washington was the first president of the U.S.A. over two hundred years ago. In like manner, one might believe that Jesus Christ lived almost two thousand years ago, having been born in Bethlehem, and crucified at Golgotha. In addition, a person might affirm the theological interpretations of Jesus' incarnation and redemptive death, but it might remain but a rationalistic mental assent to evidentiary data. Such is not the faith required for the receipt of regeneration. Biblical faith involves spiritual receptivity. Faith is our receptivity of God's activity; the receipt of the redemptive, regenerative, and restorational work of God in Jesus Christ. On many occasions when the New Testament uses the Greek word *pistis*, or the verb form *pisteuo,* it is followed by the Greek preposition *eis,* meaning "into." We might believe in, on, or about George Washington, but we do not believe "into" George Washington. On the other hand, since we are referring to spiritual reality in Jesus Christ, it can be said that we "believe into" an ontological communion with Jesus Christ as we receive His Spirit into our spirit. "As many as received Him, to them He gave the right to become children of God, even to those who believe into (*pisteuousin eis*) His name" (John 1:12). "For God so loved the world, that He gave His only begotten Son, that whoever believes into (*pisteuon eis*) Him should not perish, but have eternal life" (John 3:16). The receptivity of faith is "believing into" a connection with the very life and Being of Jesus Christ.

John explains that he wrote his gospel narrative "that you might believe that Jesus is the Christ, the Son of God; and that believing you may have life in His name" (John 20:31). The receipt of regenerative life is based upon the receptivity of faith in Jesus Christ. "Having believed, you were sealed in Him with the Holy Spirit of promise" (Eph. 1:13).

The Resource of Regeneration

The receipt of spiritual life requires a source from whence that life is drawn. It is true both physically and spiritually that one cannot give birth to himself. There must be a progenitor of the life that is given. Life cannot be derived from nothing or from a non-living source. The "personal resource" of spiritual life is the One who "is Spirit" (John 4:24), and who has "life in Himself" (John 5:26) as the "living God" (I Tim. 4:10). When Nicodemus questioned, "How can a man be born when he is old?" Jesus explained that we must be "born from above" (John 3:3), from the spiritual life of God. John writes that those who receive Jesus and become children of God are "born not of blood, nor of the will of the flesh, nor of the will of man, but of God" (John 1:13). The personal resource of life from when we receive spiritual life is God Himself. God is the progenitor of the life that we receive in regeneration.

It is also true physically and spiritually that "like begets like" in the process of the birthing of life. Since in regeneration we are "born of God" (John 1:13) and "born of the Spirit" (John 3:5,6), the life that we receive is divine life. The Christian becomes a "partaker of the divine nature" (II Peter 1:4). This does not mean that we thus have divine life inherently as God does (John 5:26), but only that we have the derived life of God within the man.

The agency of the implantation of this divine spiritual life is the Holy Spirit, using the means of the gospel of Jesus Christ. "You have been born again not of seed which is perishable but imperishable, through the living and abiding word of God" (I Peter 1:23). Jesus said that "It is the Spirit who gives life" (John 6:63), which is echoed by Paul's explanation that "the Spirit gives life" (II Cor. 3:6).

The Region of Regeneration

Where is it within the constituted levels of functionality that man needs to be renewed to life? The region where fallen man is dead is within the life-function level of his spirit. Every individual in the human race is born spiritually "dead in trespasses and sins" (Eph. 2:1,5). Such death does not imply the non-functionality of spirit, but spiritual identification with "the one having the power of death, that is the devil" (Heb. 2:14), the "personal resource of death." The need of man, therefore, is to "pass from death to life" (John 5:24; I John 3:14) spiritually in a spiritual exchange of identification and indwelling from one personal spiritual resource to the other, from Satan to God. The region of regeneration is the life-function level of the spirit.

The prophet Ezekiel served as an instrument of God's foretelling what He was going to do through His Son Jesus Christ in the new covenant. "I will put a new spirit within you. . .I will put My Spirit within you" (Ezek. 36:26,27), God said. This transpires in regeneration when the "spiritual concept" of Christ's "finished work" becomes effectual, and an individual is spiritually re-lifed. Jesus clearly specified the region of regeneration when He explained to Nicodemus that "that which is born of the Spirit is spirit" (John 3:6).

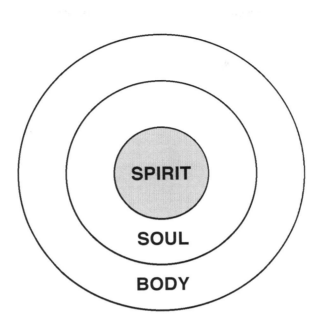

The Reposit of Regeneration

Although it has been previously indicated that the life that we receive in regeneration is the life of God, i.e. the life of Jesus Christ, it is important to emphasize that the entire life of God in His triune form is put within us and comes to dwell and live within us. The life of God the Father, Son and Holy Spirit becomes the essence of our spiritual life. This is the ontological feature of the "finished work" of Jesus Christ, whereby the Being of the triune God is restored to mankind.

God the Father dwells within the Christian. "Whoever confesses that Jesus is the Son of God, God abides in him, and he in God" (I John 4:15). To the Corinthians Paul notes that God had indicated long ago that "I will dwell in them and walk among them; and I will be their God, and they shall be My people" (II Cor. 6:16). Explaining the receptive relationship between God and the Christian, Jesus included the Father saying, "We will come to him and make Our abode with him" (John 14:23).

That Jesus Christ dwells within the Christian is abundantly documented in the New Testament Scriptures. This is the mystery of the gospel, writes Paul, "Christ in you, the hope of glory" (Col. 1:27). "It is no longer I who live, but Christ lives in me" (Gal. 2:20), he writes to the Galatians. "Do you not recognize this about yourselves, that Jesus Christ is in you?" (II Cor. 13:5), Paul asks the Corinthian Christians. John adds that, "We know that Christ abides in us, by the Spirit which He has given us" (I John 3:24). "By this we know that we abide in Christ and He in us, because He has given us of His Spirit" (I John 4:13).

The indwelling of the Holy Spirit is also amply posited by the New Testament. Paul asks the Corinthians, "Do you not know that your body is a temple of the Holy Spirit who is in you, whom you have from God?" (I Cor. 6:19). God "jealously desires the Spirit that He has made to dwell in us" (James 4:5). "Guard, through the Holy Spirit who dwells in us, the treasure which has been entrusted to you" (II Tim. 1:14).

The ontological reposit of regeneration is the divine being of Father, Son and Holy Spirit. This is the restoration of the "breath of lives" (Gen. 2:7) that God breathed into man in the garden (cf. chapter two).

The Renewal of Regeneration

To "bring into being again" by "the washing of regeneration and renewing of the Holy Spirit" (Titus 3:5), allows for a renewal of the individual that is variously described throughout the New Testament. The Christian is participating in a "new covenant" (Heb. 8:8,13), a "better covenant" (Heb. 7:22), a superior arrangement wherein God's "Laws are written in our minds and upon our hearts" (Heb 8:10; 10:16), for the presence of His being and character dwell within our spirit. It is "a new and living way which He inaugurated for us through the flesh of Jesus Christ" (Heb. 10:20), and His willingness to become humanity in order to take our death consequences and give us His life.

"If any man is in Christ, he is a new creature; the old things passed away; behold, new things have come" (II Cor. 5:17). The metaphor of "new creation" is suggested by the Greek word *genesis,* from which the English word "regeneration" is derived. Man is "re-genesized," that is, "brought into being again" in accord with God's created intent to have His life dwelling within and functioning through humanity. The real issues of Christianity are not the externalities, Paul notes, "but a new creation" (Gal. 6:15) of humanity.

The newness of humanity is effected by the "newness of life" (Rom. 6:4) that the Christian shares in identification with the resurrection of Jesus Christ, and the indwelling of His resurrection-life. By receptivity of Jesus Christ the individual becomes a "new man" (Eph. 4:24; Col. 3:10), "created in righteousness and holiness of the truth" (Eph. 4:24). The believer has a new spiritual identity as a Christ-one, a Christian.

"All things have become new" (KJV-II Cor. 5:17) for the Christian. This must be understood in reference to spiritual realities, for the patterns of fleshly behavior in the function-level of the soul are still present in recurrent conflict with the new impulses of the Spirit (Gal. 5:17).

The Relationship of Regeneration

Receiving the life of God in spiritual regeneration, the Christian has a "personal relationship" with God through the "one mediator, Jesus Christ" (I Tim. 2:5). We are "reconciled to God" (Rom. 5:10; II Cor. 5:19,20; Col. 1:20) in a spiritual oneness. "The one who joins himself to the Lord is one spirit with Him" (I Cor. 6:17).

Regeneration also creates a spiritual relationship with every other individual who has likewise received Jesus Christ. God does not intend that we become "lone ranger" Christians, isolated in individualism. Using the metaphor of birth again, it might be noted that an individual is always born into a family. The Church of Jesus Christ is the "family of God" wherein we are to relate to one another, love one another, and minister to one another. "Let us consider how to stimulate one another to love and good deeds, not forsaking our own assembling together, but encouraging one another" (Heb. 10:24,25). Within such interactive Christian fellowship the Christian individual will "grow in the grace and knowledge of our Lord Jesus Christ" (II Peter 3:18).

The Retention of Regeneration

The question of the permanency of this regenerative placement of God's life in man's spirit has long been debated. The misunderstandings often result from man's propensity to reason in strict logical categories that fail to take into account the dynamic ontological reality of the presence of God. Our security is not based on a logical positivism that results from certain receptive actions of man in a tight cause and effect procedure. Instead, our security is based on the continued faithfulness of God (I Cor. 1:9), who has no desire to renege on His express purpose to manifest His life in man. The character of God is indeed an eternal security, as He is allowed to function dynamically within mankind.

Christians can have the subjective assurance that God does indeed dwell in them. John wrote to Christians, "These things I have written to you who believe in the name of the Son of God, in order that you may know that you have eternal life" (I John 5:13). Paul noted that "The Spirit Himself bears witness with our spirit that we are children of God" (Rom. 8:16).

The Release of Regeneration

Receiving the Spirit of life into our spirit in regeneration is not an end in itself. The objective is not to "store up" the Holy Spirit in the spirit of a Christian as a "deposit" that will later be employed or "cashed in." Some Christians in their evangelistic zeal have encouraged regeneration, but never proceeded to explain what the Spirit was to do when He came to dwell in the Christian. There are Christians who have sat in their pews every Sunday for many years, and heard sermon after sermon on "What it means to be 'Born Again'," but have never been taught concerning the Spirit's continued activity. This phenomena is oftentimes a result of an eschatological futurism that projects all the benefits of Jesus Christ into the heavenly future and has no expectation for the effectiveness of His life in the world today. It is tragic that many Christians conceive of the Christian life as "the past is forgiven; the future is assured; but the present is the pits!"

Regeneration is a crisis with a view to a process. At a particular point in time the Spirit of Christ takes up residence in the spirit of an individual who receives Him by faith. "If anyone does not have the Spirit of Christ, he does not belong

149

to Him" (Rom. 8:9). The Spirit of Christ in the spirit of the Christian is not "on hold" until we get to heaven. God's intent is that the life of Jesus Christ be released into behavioral expression. This is the "functional concept" of His "finished work." The derivation of spiritual condition must lead to the derivation of behavioral expression. Regeneration must extend into sanctification. The writer to the Hebrews admonishes, "Let us press on to maturity" (Heb. 6:1).

When the "personal resource" of Christ's life is received into the spirit of man at regeneration, the "prevailing ramifications" of that life are to become behaviorally operative expressing the character of God, and allowing for a "perpetual representation" of ontological union of life in Jesus Christ. To the Galatians, Paul wrote, "It is no longer I who lives, but Christ lives in me, and the life that I now live in the flesh I live by faith in the Son of God" (Gal. 2:20). To the Corinthians, he explained that the objective was that "the life of Jesus might be manifested in our body...in our mortal flesh" (II Cor. 4:10,11). The life of Jesus Christ must be released in order to be manifested in the Christian's behavior, to be lived out to the glory of God.

The Results of Regeneration

The apostle John in his typical "black and white" thinking, explains particular behavioral manifestations that should be indicative of one who has been regenerated and received the divine life within:

"You know that every one who practices righteousness is born of Him" (I John 2:29). Those in whom the "Righteous One" (Acts 3:14; 7:52; 22:14) dwells and lives will derive His righteous character in righteous behavior. There is no other way to manifest righteousness except as derived from

150

Christ, for all other feeble attempts at such are as a "filthy rag" (Isa. 64:6) and to be "counted as rubbish" (Phil. 3:8). The character of righteousness in our behavior will be a result of the regeneration whereby "Jesus Christ, the Righteous" (I John 2:1) comes to live in us and manifest His life through us.

"We know that we have passed out of death into life, because we love the brethren. He who does not love abides in death" (I John 3:14). "God is love" (I John 4:8,16), and when He comes to dwell in us at regeneration, the manifestations of His loving character, the "fruit of the Spirit which is love..." (Gal. 5:22,23), should be expressed behaviorally. "The love of God has been poured out within our hearts through the Holy Spirit who was given to us" (Rom. 5:5).

"No one who is born of God practices sin, because His seed abides in him; and he cannot sin, because he is born of God" (I John 3:9). This verse has spawned numerous perfectionistic theses, but the meaning seems to be that the Perfect One, Jesus Christ, comes to live in the Christian at regeneration. As the "Sinless One" (II Cor. 5:21; I Peter 2:22), He does not sin, nor tempt us to sin (James 1:13). An individual in whom Christ dwells should desire that the character of Christ be derivatively expressed in his behavior, repudiating the sinful expressions that are contrary to His character. Realism forces us to remember that "If we say that we have no sin, we are deceiving ourselves, and the truth is not in us" (I John 1:8).

"Whatever is born of God overcomes the world; and who is the one who overcomes the world, but he who believes that Jesus is the Son of God" (I John 5:4,5). Jesus is the Overcomer who has "overcome the world" (John 16:33). When He comes to live in us at regeneration, He is the sufficient spiritual provision for the overcoming of Satan's world-system with all its evil influences and sin. "Greater is He who is in you, than he who is in the world" (I John 4:4). "The Lamb will overcome, because He is Lord of Lords and King of Kings" (Rev. 17:14).

"We know that no one who is born of God sins; but He who was born of God keeps him and the evil one does not touch him" (I John 5:18). Again, the Sinless One, Jesus Christ, who has come to live in us at regeneration, does not sin or prompt us to sin. He also "protects us from the Evil One" (II Thess. 3:3) by "the power of God" (I Peter 1:5), "not allowing us to be tempted beyond what we are able" (I Cor. 10:13). Christians are thus empowered by the indwelling Christ for the avoidance of temptation as "He comes to the aid of those who are tempted" (Heb. 2:18).

The results of regeneration will be the expression of God's character in the behavior of man. God's intent in the reinvestiture of His life in man through the work of His Son Jesus Christ was that man might function as God had originally intended by allowing the life and character of God to be expressed in man's behavior to the glory of God. Only when the life of God is "brought into being again" by spiritual regeneration in man, is the divine dynamic present in man whereby he might derive from God and express godly character. Regeneration is necessary if man is to be man as God intended man to be.

9

The Fullness of God in Man

The new spiritual condition of the regenerated individual is not an end in itself. Regeneration is a punctiliar event with a view to the process of allowing the divine character now indwelling the spirit of the Christian to be expressed behaviorally. The "personal resource of life," the presence of the Spirit of Christ, must now be allowed to exhibit the "prevailing ramifications" of His life, the "life of Jesus manifested in our mortal bodies" (II Cor. 4:10,11).

In terms of our spiritual condition, it can be said that the Christian is "complete in Christ" (Col. 2:10). "All things have been made new" (II Cor. 5:17) in our spirit because the Spirit of Christ dwells therein constituting us a "new man" (Eph. 4:24; Col. 3:10). We have "every spiritual blessing in heavenly places in Christ" (Eph. 1:3); "all things pertaining to life and godliness" (II Peter 1:3). "Of His fullness we have all received" (John 1:16), the "fullness of the blessing of Christ" (Rom. 15:29), whereby we are "full of goodness" (Rom. 15:14) and "full of the gladness of His presence" (Acts 2:28).

Though every Christian is spiritually full of the presence of the Spirit of Christ, for "He gives the Spirit without measure" (John 3:34), the process of allowing the life and character of Christ to fill and pervade our mental, emotional and

153

volitional activities in order to be expressed in the behavior of our bodies continues as a constant necessity for the remainder of our lives here on earth. Paul's prayer for the Ephesians, though they participated in "the fullness of Him who fills all in all" (Eph. 1:23), was that they might "be filled up to all the fullness of God" (Eph. 3:19), "to the measure of the stature which belongs to the fullness of Christ" (Eph. 4:13). Such is the basis of our consideration of the fullness of God in man.

Consideration of the release of the Spirit of Christ into behavioral expression using the figure of being "filled with the Spirit" has long been clouded with misunderstandings and extremisms, controversy and confusion. Biblical phraseology utilizes metaphors that portray the action of the Spirit in liquid terms such as "rivers of living water" (John 7:38) and the Spirit being "poured out" (Acts 2:17) upon mankind. Some have conceived of an external application of the Spirit's activity such as filling their tank with a liquid petroleum product in order to provide power for locomotion. Others have conceptualized God as a "cosmic waiter" with a big pitcher of liquid Holy Spirit, and they are petitioning God to "fill their cup." These conceptions err in representing an additional external application of the Spirit subsequent to the Christian's receiving the Spirit of Christ internally at regeneration. Since "all spiritual things belong to us in Christ" (I Cor. 3:21,22), to suggest that the Christian needs something more is to suggest that Jesus Christ is insufficient. A more adequate and accurate picture is to recognize that the Christian has received the Spirit of Christ in his spirit at regeneration (Rom. 8:9) and is "complete in Christ" (Col. 2:10). Internally, from the inside out, the Spirit of Christ functions like an artesian well "springing up to eternal life" (John 4:14), to fill our behavior with His character and to overflow in ministry unto others.

Paul's command to the Ephesians will serve as a primary text for the study of the filling of the Spirit unto the fullness of God in man. "Do not get drunk with wine, for that is dissipation, but be filled with the Spirit" (Eph. 5:18).

The Context of the Filling

The context in which Paul's command is stated within the epistle to the Ephesians has to do with practical behavior. Referring to the conduct of daily life, Paul admonishes the Ephesian Christians to "be careful how you walk" (Eph. 5:15) so as to be "wise" and "make the most of your time" (Eph. 5:16). It is important, Paul says, to "understand what the will of the Lord is" (Eph. 5:17), which is always the expression of the character of Jesus Christ. The context of the filling of the Spirit is not an ecstatic or esoteric experience wherein one is zapped by God, nor is it a mystical mood-altering manifestation. Rather, the filling of the Spirit relates to intensely practical behavior.

In like manner as the foregoing context, the context which follows Paul's command in Ephesians 5:18 also relates to practical behavior. The results of being thus filled with the Spirit will be a "song in your heart" (Eph. 5:19), a thankful attitude (Eph. 5:20), and deference to one another in interpersonal relationships (Eph. 5:21). Can anything be more practical than behavior which exhibits the character of Christ within husband and wife relationships (Eph. 5:22-33), parent and child relationships (Eph. 6:1-4), and employer and employee relationships (Eph. 6:5-9)? In such relationships God wants to see the fullness of his character expressed in the behavior of Christians.

The Command of the Filling

When Paul commands the Ephesian Christians to "be filled with the Spirit," the verb is in an imperative mood. This is not something that is an optional extra in the Christian life, but is to be regarded as obligatory. It is not something that we can pick or choose, take or leave, in terms of Christian obedience. It is a mandate.

Closer examination reveals two commands in Ephesians 5:18. The first command is "Do not get drunk." If the number of messages and treatises on a particular text reveals the priority of such, then I would venture to presume that the majority of expositors and preachers have regarded this command as the one of predominant importance in this verse, for the inculcations of temperance have been most abundant. Far fewer have been the practical instructions concerning what it means to "be filled with the Spirit." It seems to be the propensity of man to focus and fixate on the negative admonitions rather than the positive admonitions, failing to recognize that the positive admonitions usually encompass the negative. For example, if we are "being transformed by the renewing of our mind" this will inclusively forestall our "being conformed to this world" (Rom. 12:2). Likewise, if the Christian is being "filled with the Spirit," such will serve to forestall his "being drunk with wine." To over-emphasize the behavioral modifications of nonconformity or abstinence in these verses is to evade the grace of God which is to be found in the divine empowering of mental renewal and the control of the Spirit. In both of these instances the positive and negative commands must be held together.

Many Christians seem to be quite adamant in their insistence on abstinence or temperance concerning wine and alcoholic beverages. Are they as adamant in their insistence upon being filled with the Spirit? If not, then why the inconsistency? It should be as inappropriate for you to not be filled with the Spirit right now, as it would be for you to be getting drunk right now!

The Compass of the Filling

To whom does this command extend? Is this command to "be filled with the Spirit" meant for every Christian? Some seem to think that to "be filled with the Spirit" is an experience that is reserved for a privileged few in the Church, that it is a deluxe edition of the Christian life meant for super-Christians, perhaps those involved as missionaries, pastors or church leaders. This is not the case.

When Paul commands the Ephesian Christians to "be filled with the Spirit," there is an implied subject that must be ascertained from the verb. The verb "be filled" is second-person plural in number, which means that we can supply the subject as "you all." "You all be filled with the Spirit," commands Paul, or if he were in the southern part of the United States he might say, "Y'all be filled with the Spirit." The filling of the Spirit is meant for all Christians. All Christians are responsible to individually allow for this activity of the Spirit of Christ in their lives. The plural subject does not allow for a corporate application, as some have suggested, any more than the correlative command "not to get drunk" allows for a corporate application.

To be filled with the Spirit is the birthright of every Christian. Having been "born of the Spirit" (John 3:5,6), we are to be "filled with the Spirit." Many Christians, like Esau (Gen. 25:34), seem to be despising their birthright, willing to sell it for a mess of pottage and temporary indulgence. God intends for every Christian to "be filled with the Spirit," for such is the normal Christian life wherein man functions as God intended man to function.

The Comparison of the Filling

When Paul uses the concepts of "getting drunk with wine" and "being filled with the Spirit" in the same sentence, he is obviously making some kind of comparison by way of contrast. This is not the only occasion in Scripture where these two concepts are used in conjunction with one another. Luke records that Zacharias heard an angel indicate that his son, John the Baptist, "would drink no wine or liquor, but would be filled with the Holy Spirit" (Luke 1:15). Later Luke would record that on Pentecost the apostles were "filled with the Holy Spirit" (Acts 2:4), and observers mocked them, saying, "They are full of sweet wine" (Acts 2:13).

What do these two concepts have in common that would cause Paul to employ them in contrastual comparison? When a person is drunk it is usually obvious from the way he behaves. He does not need a sign hanging around his neck which reads, "I am drunk!" His drunkenness is evident from the way he walks, thinks, talks and relates to other people. The alcohol affects his feet, his mind, his tongue, and his relationships. Interestingly enough, in the immediate context of his command, Paul refers to being "careful how you walk" (Eph. 5:15), being "wise" and "understanding" (Eph. 5:15,17), indicating that "being filled with the Spirit" will affect your "speaking to one another" (Eph. 5:19) and your relationships (Eph. 5:22-6:9). The effects of being filled with the Spirit, like those of getting drunk, will affect one's walk, thought, talk and relationships.

The process of getting drunk and being filled with the Spirit also have some similarities. There is nothing mysterious or mystical about getting drunk. A person simply consumes enough alcohol until they are captivated, motivated and activated by the alcoholic "spirits." In a similar manner the Christian makes a choice to allow himself to be captivated, motivated and activated by the Holy Spirit. The comparison that Paul is making then becomes obvious: "Do not be captivated, motivated and activated by the alcoholic spirits, but be captivated, motivated and activated by the Holy Spirit." Alcohol has often been identified with "spirits" that are in contrast to the Spirit of God, even referred to as "the demon in the bottle." There are many forms of intoxication, though, which can captivate, motivate and activate human behavior. People can be intoxicated with politics, business, entertainment, even their "wife's breasts" (Prov. 5:19) and sexuality. Christians are not to abandon themselves in excess, dissipation or debauchery to any object or activity, but are to submit to the personal activity of the Spirit of Christ.

The Concept of the Filling

The contrasted comparison of "getting drunk" and "being filled with the Spirit" provides us with a basic concept of what it means to "be filled with the Spirit." The basic concept is that of an individual being controlled by a substance or another being. Paul is commanding us, "Do not be controlled by alcoholic spirits, but be controlled by the Holy Spirit." "Do not be under the influence of the alcoholic spirits, but be under the influence of the Holy Spirit." "Do not abandon your personality to the alcoholic substance, but voluntarily surrender your behavior to the Lordship of the Spirit of Christ."

As dependent, contingent and derivative creatures, we will always be controlled by a spirit-being other than ourselves. Man never operates in a spiritual vacuum. God's intent is that Christians who have received the Spirit of Christ into their spirit (Rom. 8:9) should allow "the Lord who is the Spirit" (II Cor. 3:17,18; Rom. 1:4) to control their behavior at each moment in time so as to allow the divine character to be expressed in their behavior to the glory of God (I Cor. 10:31).

The Consignor of the Filling

Since we are derivative beings, the controlling activity of "being filled with the Spirit" is not something that is autonomous and self-generated. It is not the activity of self-effort coming from within ourselves. "Not that we are adequate to consider anything as coming from ourselves, but our adequacy is of God" (II Cor. 3:5). There is a divine consignor who supplies, conveys, dispatches, delivers and imparts this controlling activity within the Christian. It is not an attainment, but an obtainment derived from the ontological presence of God within the spirit of the Christian.

When Paul commands that we "be filled with the Spirit," the Greek verb that he employs is in the passive voice. This does not mean that the Christian is a passive object, unengaged in the process of "being filled with the Spirit." It is not a process of being passively controlled by another, as in a hypnotic trance. A person does not get drunk passively, but by actively partaking of the alcoholic beverage. The Christian, exercising his faculties of choice, voluntarily surrenders to the control of God's Spirit, receptive to God's activity in his behavior. The passive voice in the Greek language indicates that the subject of the verb is being acted upon. The understood subject is "you all," and the One who is to be allowed to act upon the freely chosen behavior of all Christians is God the Father, Son and Holy Spirit.

160

The Content of the Filling

God is not only the supplier of the activity of the filling of the Spirit, but that which He supplies is the ontological activity of His own Being, expressive of His own character. The Spirit of God is both the giver and the gift. This is why the Greek preposition *en* which Paul uses when he commands us to "be filled with the Spirit" is alternately translated both as "be filled *by* the Spirit" and "be filled *with* the Spirit." The Holy Spirit enacts the process of the filling, and in so doing fills us with Himself.

Many of the misunderstandings of what is involved in the "filling of the Spirit," stem from a truncated theological understanding of the triune Godhead. The ontological content of the filling of the Spirit involves the divine activity of the Father, Son and Holy Spirit. They function only in their triunity as the Spirit of God, the Spirit of Christ, and the Holy Spirit. Attempts to force separated function within the trinity of the Godhead will inevitably lead to perverted understanding of God's activity within the Christian.

Reiteratively, it should also be noted that the content of this filling activity does not imply or involve the supplying of any additional divine substance. God and His activity are a unity that cannot be fragmented. "He gives the Spirit without measure" (John 3:34). The Christian is "complete in Christ" (Col. 2:10), having "every spiritual blessing in heavenly places in Christ Jesus" (Eph. 1:3). To be filled with the Spirit is not our receiving more of the Holy Spirit, but the Holy Spirit being allowed to have more control of our behavior.

The Continuity of the Filling

The activity of being filled or controlled by the Spirit of God is not a singular, static, once-and-for-all experience. It is not an existential event that we forever look back on, remembering its impact on our life. It is not a "filling" of yesteryear that imparts to the Christian a level of spirituality, never to be diminished or forsaken.

Previously we noted that regeneration is the punctiliar crisis that is designed to lead to the process of allowing the risen Lord Jesus to control our behavioral expression as Christians. When Paul commanded that we "be filled with the Spirit," the verb that he used was in the present tense. This can be translated and interpreted as a continuous present tense wherein we are to "be continuously being filled with the Spirit." To the woman at the well in Samaria, Jesus explained that, "The water I shall give will become a spring of water welling up to eternal life" (John 4:14). There is nothing static about a spring of water. It is ever-active. The dynamic of Christ's life operative in the behavior of the Christian is to be continuously allowed to function. How does a person who is drunk stay drunk? He must continue to partake of the alcohol. Likewise, the Christian must continue to be receptive to the activity of the Spirit of God.

At one moment in time we might be filled and controlled by the Holy Spirit, and at the next moment in time we might fail to be so filled. As we respond to the circumstances of life, there is always the temptation to act and react in ways that do not evidence the control of the Spirit and the conveyance of divine character. The toilet stops up and runs over. A child drops a piece of china or knocks over an expensive lamp. We lock our keys in the car, or discover we have a flat tire. Our spouse does something we do not appreciate. At those moments in time are we faithfully receptive to the control of God's Spirit in our behavior? Being filled with the Spirit involves the continuous, moment-by-moment availability to the dynamic activity of God expressing His character through our behavior in every situation.

The Connotations of the Filling

A study of the New Testament usages where the action of "filling" is used in reference to the Spirit, reveals that there are various connotations of the manner in which Christians are controlled by the Spirit and the results of such. The different connotations can be ascertained by the three different Greek words that are used, even though they are all derived from a common root.

By utilizing Ephesians 5:18 as our primary text so far in this study, we have been considering what might be called "the filling of progressive possession." The Greek word used in this verse is the verb *pleroo,* which refers to the general action of filling up. When used in reference to the activity of the Holy Spirit, it implies the moment-by-moment control of the Spirit in Christian behavior. The same Greek verb is used in Acts 13:52 where it is reported that "the disciples were continually filled with joy and with the Holy Spirit."

The "filling of progressive possession" is intended to become a "predominant pattern" of fullness in the Christian life. When such Spirit-control of one's behavior becomes an abiding pattern in one's life, that individual might be referred to as a "Spirit-filled person." Thus it is that the New Testament uses the Greek adjective *pleres* to refer to an individual whose lifestyle was characterized by such control. Jesus was obviously "full of the Holy Spirit" (Luke 4:1), even in the wilderness when being tempted by the devil. The seven servers selected by the early Church were to be "full of the Holy Spirit and of wisdom" (Acts 6:3). Stephen was one of the seven who was "full of faith and of the Holy Spirit" (Acts 6:5), and he remained so when being martyred (Acts 7:55). Barnabas is also characterized as being "a good man, and full of the Holy Spirit and of faith" (Acts 11:24). Their lifestyle was characterized by a "predominating pattern" of allowing the Spirit of Christ to be in control of their behavior. This does not mean that these individuals, with the exception of Jesus, were being filled in an absolute sense so as to be without sin. The use of this adjective described their overall behavior as having the governing disposition and abiding characteristic of the Spirit's control. Only Jesus Himself was totally controlled by God the Father in the man, so as to function perfectly for every moment in time for thirty-three years "without sin" (Heb. 4:15).

On several occasions throughout the New Testament the Holy Spirit is reported to have controlled a person's behavior in the sense of a "productive power" for an assignment of divine service. Whenever this sense of the Spirit's filling control is mentioned, the Greek verb *pimplemi* is employed. This refers to a specific action of filling for a particular result. In every case the particular ministry involves a verbal witness of God's action in Jesus Christ. John the Baptist, the "voice crying in the wilderness" (Luke 3:4), was to be "filled with the Holy Spirit, while yet in his mother's womb" (Luke 1:15), set apart for a particular ministry of witness as a forerunner to foretell of the Messiah, Jesus Christ. John's mother, Elizabeth, was "filled with the Holy Spirit" (Luke 1:41) and cried out with a loud voice exclaiming the blessing of the One who was yet in the womb of Mary. John's father, Zacharias, "was filled with the Holy Spirit, and prophesied" (Luke 1:67) of the salvation that was to come in Jesus Christ.

After Jesus had come and had ascended, the Holy Spirit was "poured out" on Pentecost, and the disciples were "filled with the Holy Spirit and began to speak with other tongues, as the Spirit was giving them utterance" (Acts 2:4), which allowed foreigners to "hear in the language to which they were born" (Acts 2:8). Peter was "filled with the Holy Spirit" (Acts 4:8) in order to speak before Annas, Caiaphas and those of high-priestly descent. Paul was "filled with the Holy Spirit" (Acts 9:17) for a particular ministry of productive power as an apostle to the Gentiles, and spoke boldly before Sergius Paulus (Acts 13:9). Many Christians were "filled with the Holy Spirit, and began to speak the word of God with boldness" (Acts 4:31) after Peter and John were released from prison. Notice how all of these references explain the control of the Spirit for a productive power of verbal witness.

Each of the connotations of the filling of the Spirit pertain to the control of God's Spirit whether moment-by-moment, habitually, or for a particular ministry. The moment-by-moment filling of "progressive possession" should become the "predominant pattern" of fullness in every Christian, and we might all have particular fillings of "productive power" for witnessing in particular circumstances. The continuous Christocentric control of the Spirit should issue forth in consistent character which will lend credence to the circumstantial competency of controlled ministry.

The Contradictions of the Filling

What keeps Christians from being filled or controlled by the Spirit of Christ? Several phrases are used throughout the Scriptures to refer to actions which contradict the intended control of the Spirit:

Resisting the Spirit. When Stephen made his defense before the Jerusalem Council, he said to the religious leaders, "You men who are stiff-necked and uncircumcised in heart and ears are always resisting the Holy Spirit" (Acts 7:51). Those to whom Stephen spoke were unregenerate Jewish leaders, but the action of resisting the Spirit's activity in our lives is of sufficient breadth to apply to Christians also.

Quenching the Spirit. Writing to the Thessalonians, Paul admonishes the Christians there, "Do not quench the Spirit" (I Thess. 5:19). The imagery used here is that of putting out the fire of the Spirit. It is a sin of omission when the Christian disallows the Spirit of Christ to provide the impulse and the energizing of His activity in our behavior. Oftentimes the Christian selectively determines which areas of his life the Spirit of God will be allowed to control, and quenches divine activity in other areas.

Grieving the Spirit. The Holy Spirit of God is personally grieved when a Christian chooses to engage in behavior which is contrary to the character of God. Such a sin of commission makes the Spirit sorrowful. God's people of the old covenant "rebelled and grieved His Holy Spirit" (Isa. 63:10), whereupon He became their enemy. Paul warns Christians, "Do not grieve the Holy Spirit of God, by whom you were sealed for the day of redemption" (Eph. 4:30). The context of Paul's remarks indicate that the commission of the sins of bitterness, wrath, anger, clamoring, slander, malice, etc., which are contrary to God's character, are representative of the sins which grieve the Spirit.

166

Lying to the Spirit. When Ananias and Sapphira conspired to withhold some of the sale of their property, and misrepresent themselves as having given everything, Peter confronted Ananias, saying, "Ananias, why has Satan filled your heart to lie to the Holy Spirit?" (Acts 5:3). God is omniscient, and knows our hearts. Whenever Christians attempt to give the false impression that they have a "spirituality" that exceeds that of others, and are "holier than thou," they are likely to be exposed in their masquerade.

Testing the Spirit. In the same narrative referred to above, Peter confronts Sapphira, who was not aware of what had happened to her husband, saying, "Why is it that you have agreed together to put the spirit of the Lord to the test?" (Acts 5:9). Though the King James Version translates this verse as "tempting the Spirit," James has written that "God cannot be tempted" (James 1:13), so it is advisable to translate this as "testing the Spirit." Christians test the Holy Spirit whenever they engage in activity that is not derived from the energizing of the Spirit, and question whether the Spirit really knows their hearts.

Defiling the temple of the Spirit. When an individual is regenerated and indwelt by the Holy Spirit, his body serves as the exterior temple in which God dwells. Paul argues that immorality and impurity expressed in the body are misrepresentative of the character of the One who lives within, and is thus a defilement of the instrument or house in which God dwells. "Do you not know that your body is a temple of the Holy Spirit who is in you, whom you have from God, and that you are not your own? For you have been bought with a price; therefore glorify God in your body" (I Cor. 6:19,20).

Insulting the Spirit. When a Christian stands against the Savior he has received and apostatizes from faith in Jesus Christ, he is obviously not controlled by the Spirit, and such is an "insult to the Spirit of grace" (Heb. 10:29).

Blaspheming the Spirit. Attributing Christ's activity to that of Satan (Mark 3:22-30) is never the controlling activity of the Holy Spirit, for the Spirit always glorifies Christ (John 16:14). To speak against the Spirit of God and blaspheme Him is unforgivable (Matt. 12:32).

All of the foregoing contradictions to being filled with the Spirit of Christ are failures to allow for the receptivity of the Spirit's activity in human lives.

The Contrast of the Filling

To consider and compare other Biblical phrases which refer to the activity of the Holy Spirit with the action of the Spirit's filling and controlling the Christian individual will serve to better describe and define what is meant by the Spirit's filling.

Born of the Spirit. When Jesus advised Nicodemus of the necessity of being "born of the Spirit" (John 3:4,5,8), He was speaking of the need of mankind to be "brought into being again" with spiritual life. The "Spirit of life in Christ Jesus" (Rom. 8:2) comes to dwell in the spirit of an individual who is receptive by faith. "If any man does not have the Spirit of Christ, he is none of His" (Rom. 8:9). "By the washing of regeneration and the renewing of the Holy Spirit" (Titus 3:5), an individual is constituted a Christian.

Receiving the Spirit. The receiving of the Spirit of Christ (Acts 2:38) into the spirit of a man at regeneration is the necessary spiritual reality of becoming a Christian. Without such, an individual is not yet considered a Christian (Acts 19:2). John explained that Jesus had referred to "the Spirit, whom those who believed in Him were to receive" (John 7:39).

Indwelling of the Spirit. Jesus told His disciples that in His physical absence, "the Spirit of Truth will be in you" (John 14:17). Jesus Christ "abides in us, by the Spirit which He has given us" (I John 3:24). When we are regenerated the "Spirit indwells us" (Rom. 8:11), and we must "guard through the Holy Spirit who dwells in us, the treasure which has been entrusted to us" (II Tim. 1:14).

Gift of the Spirit. In the first sermon of the early church Peter explained that by responding to Jesus Christ "you shall receive the gift of the Holy Spirit" (Acts 2:38). That gift is the presence of the Holy Spirit Himself "Who was given to us" (Rom. 5:5) at regeneration.

Seal of the Spirit. In Biblical times a "seal" represented a mark of ownership, a seal of security, a finished transaction. All of these figures become true for us spiritually when we receive the Spirit of Christ in regeneration. "Having believed, we were sealed in Him with the Holy Spirit of promise" (Eph. 1:13), "the Holy Spirit of God in whom we were sealed for the day of redemption" (Eph. 4:30). "God has sealed us and gave us the Spirit in our hearts as a pledge" (II Cor. 1:21,22).

Anointing of the Spirit. Throughout the old covenant priests and kings were anointed to express their place of service among God's people. A spiritual anointing is predicated of all regenerated believers in the new covenant, for we are a "kingdom of priests" (Rev. 1:6) in the "royal priesthood" (I Peter 2:9) of God's new people. "He who establishes us in Christ and anointed us is God" (II Cor. 1:21). "We have an anointing from the Holy One" (I John 2:20); "the anointing which you received from Him abides in you, and...His anointing teaches you about all things" (I John 2:27), just as Jesus said the Spirit would do (John 14:26).

Baptism in the Spirit. In each of the four gospel narratives John the Baptist points to Jesus as the One who will not only baptize with water, but will "baptize in the Holy Spirit" (Matt. 3:11; Mark 1:8; Luke 3:16; John 1:33). Just prior to His ascension Jesus reiterated John's prophecy, saying to His disciples, "John baptized with water, but you shall be baptized with the Holy Spirit not many days from now" (Acts 1:5), the fulfillment of which transpired on Pentecost. When Peter was called to report to the Council at Jerusalem and justify what happened at the house of Cornelius when Gentiles were first regenerated, he explains that "the Holy Spirit fell upon them, just as He did upon us at the beginning (i.e. at Pentecost), and I remembered the word of the Lord, how He used to say, 'John baptized with water, but you shall be baptized with the Holy Spirit'" (Acts 11:15,16). The uniqueness of the Spirit of God overwhelming the spirit of an individual in regeneration was regarded as the mark of God's spiritual activity in the new covenant era, and the universality of such was illustrated both for Jews at Pentecost (Acts 2:1-13) and for Gentiles in Caesarea (Acts 10:34-48). To the Corinthians Paul writes, "For we were all baptized into one body by one

Spirit, whether Jews or Greeks, ...and were all made to drink of one Spirit" (I Cor. 12:13). In the context of emphasizing the universality of the new covenant spiritual reality, Paul notes that every Christian whose spirit has been baptized or overwhelmed by the Spirit of God in regeneration has been made to partake of the Holy Spirit and is a part of the spiritual Body of Christ, the Church.

Filling of the Spirit. What, then, is the difference between these foregoing activities of the Holy Spirit, and the "filling of the Spirit?" While the foregoing activities all relate in some manner to the receipt of the Holy Spirit at regeneration, the "filling of the Spirit" pertains to the subsequent activity of the Spirit in the Christian's life as he allows the Spirit of Christ to control his behavioral expression. It might be said that the foregoing activities of the Spirit refer to that time when the Spirit of God becomes resident in our lives, but the "filling of the Spirit" refers to that process of allowing the Spirit to become president of our lives, i.e. to allow Jesus Christ to exercise His Lordship in our lives.

At regeneration the Spirit of God comes to indwell our spirit, making us "partakers of His divine nature" (II Peter 1:4), and causing us to become "new men" (Eph. 4:24; Col. 3:10) with a new identity as "Christ-ones," Christians. The Spirit must then be allowed to move out and influence and control our behavior in every area of our lives.

171

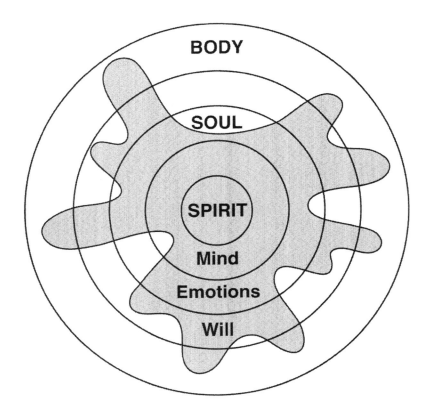

The foregoing diagram attempts to illustrate how the Holy Spirit Who occupies the Christian's spirit at regeneration should be allowed to move out and influence our Christian behavior psychologically and physically. From the inside out the Spirit of Christ desires to control our thinking, our affections, our decisions, and the actions of our bodies in order to manifest His character in all that we do. In some areas of our lives we might be allowing this to happen more than in other areas of our lives. If the circle were divided in slices like a pie, the shaded area might extend further in some areas than in others, whether it be our family life, social life, personal relationships, business, health, education, recreation, sports, sexuality, driving habits, etc. To what extent is the Spirit of Christ being allowed to control our thinking, affections, decisions and actions in each of these areas? The "battle-front" in the spiritual warfare of our Christian lives could be represented as the outer line of the shaded area. It is there that the struggle continues as to whether we will allow Christ to fill and control our behavior with His life and character, or whether we will be filled with behavior contrary to the character of Christ, i.e. sin. John reminds us that, "Greater is He who is in you, than he who is in the world" (I John 4:4).

One person observed that the shaded area of this illustration is like a "sanctification blob," meaning that it is ever-changing as we allow the holy character of God to be evidenced in our behavior. The outside of the shaded area might also be referred to as "the growing edge" of our Christian lives as we seek to "grow in the grace and knowledge of our Lord and Savior Jesus Christ" (II Peter 3:18). As with every two-dimensional illustration, this one also has its limitations in representing the complexities of human function.

The Commencement of the Filling

When is the process of being "filled with the Spirit" supposed to begin in the Christian life? Many persons have been regenerated and become Christians, but have never been advised of their birthright for allowing the life of Jesus Christ to be lived out in their behavior. In their evangelistic zeal many evangelical Christian preachers and teachers have so emphasized regeneration and being "born again" to the neglect of explaining the on-going expression of Christ's life. Because of this inadequacy of Christian instruction many Christians have proceeded down the road of their Christian

173

lives for many years before they ever come to the realization of God's intent in their lives. Then, by hearing another speaker, reading a book, or by the personal enlightenment of the Holy Spirit in reading the Scriptures, they recognize that the life of Jesus Christ which was born in them is designed to be lived out through them. What a revelation! Many explain that it was at a point of desperation when they despaired of ever being able to live the Christian life in the midst of the circumstances that confronted them, that the critical "turning point" or "crisis" came and they realized that the grace of God was sufficient to be filled and controlled by the Holy Spirit for the outliving of Christ's life. The point of recognition for many of these Christians can be such a traumatic experience that they are more excited and exhilarated than they were when they were first regenerated. Some of them refer to this experience as "a second work of grace" subsequent to regeneration, and seek to standardize the phenomena in the lives of all Christians. Some refer to such an experience as "the baptism of the Holy Spirit," for it seems that the Holy Spirit began to overwhelm their lives from that point onward. Semantic misunderstanding and confusion of nomenclature has resulted. Despite the differing terminology utilized in fundamentalist, holiness and Pentecostal circles, our desire should be to see the life of Jesus Christ lived out in Christian behavior to the glory of God, regardless of how it is labeled.

The commencement of the filling of the Spirit should immediately follow the regeneration of the Spirit. Having come to live in us spiritually, Christ wants to live His life out through us behaviorally. By the filling-control of the Spirit, Jesus wants to function as Lord in our lives. New Christians should be instructed and advised of the grace and sufficiency of Jesus Christ, so that they can enter into the Spirit-filled lifestyle as soon as possible after regeneration, and glorify God thereby.

The Conditions of the Filling

How does the Christian allow for the filling of the Holy Spirit so that Christ can control the conduct and behavior of his life? Is there anything that we have to do in order to effect this result? Are there procedures and techniques and formulas that will cause this to take place in our lives, as the abundance of "how to" books available today seem to advocate?

Paul simply tells the Colossians, "As you therefore have received Christ Jesus the Lord, so walk in Him, having been firmly rooted, built up in Him and established in your faith" (Col. 2:6). How did we receive Christ Jesus initially? By faith, our receptivity of His remedial, redemptive and restorative activity on our behalf. How then are we to continue to walk in the Christian life? By faith, our receptivity of His activity of expressing His life through our behavior. Everything in the Christian life is "by grace through faith" (Eph. 2:8), not a result of human "works" of which we might boast (Eph. 2:9). Paul chides and chastises the Galatians, asking, "Did you receive the Spirit by works... or by hearing with faith? Having begun by the Spirit, are you now being perfected by the flesh?" (Gal. 3:2,3). "We receive the promise of the Spirit through faith" (Gal. 3:14), and in like manner we receive everything necessary for the living of the Christian life by grace through faith. The Christian life is not lived by the works of human effort, by going through various motions and rituals, by keeping certain rules and regulations, by mustering up more commitment and dedication. The Christian life is lived only by Jesus Christ as He is allowed to fill and control our behavior. Jesus said, "Apart from Me, you can do nothing" (John 15:5). Paul further explains that "God is at work in you, both to will and to work for His good pleasure" (Phil. 2:13). By faith we are receptive to His activity of filling and control in our behavior.

In similar manner as we responded in faith for regeneration (cf. pages 124-134), the Christian *believes* that this is what Christ wants to do in living His life out through us. His emotions have *godly sorrow* for any misrepresentations of sin in his life. There is an ongoing decision of *repentance* as our minds are changed to receptive availability in order to allow for the changed action of the derived dynamic of divine activity. There will then be the *confession* of a behavioral lifestyle that evidences the life of Jesus Christ. The Christian life is not what we do, but what we allow Jesus Christ to do through us by faith.

The Consequences of the Filling

Are there particular results of being "filled with the Spirit" that can or should be identified? Oftentimes Christians have arbitrarily determined criteria by which they seek to evaluate whether others have been, or are being, filled with the Spirit. Such man-made criteria are dangerous and divisive.

Jesus Christ will express Himself uniquely in every Christian individual. It is not for the Christian community to seek to stereotype and standardize His expressions. Our focus should be on the manifestation of Jesus Christ, not on particular behavioral manifestations such as "speaking in tongues" or having a particular "second blessing experience." We should not seek to emulate how Jesus Christ chooses to express Himself in another Christian.

There are two general areas, though, where the consequences of the filling of the Spirit will be evident:

When the Spirit of Christ is allowed to control our behavior, the *character* of Christ will be evidenced. "The fruit of the Spirit is love, joy, peace, patience, kindness, goodness, faithfulness, gentleness, godly self-control" (Gal. 5:22,23). Jesus did seem to indicate that "by their fruit you will know them" (Matt. 7:16,20; 12:33), but this does not necessarily mean that we should set ourselves up as "fruit-inspectors" to determine whether others are being filled by the Spirit. It will eventually be obvious for all to see whether we have the practical expressions of a song in our heart, a thankful attitude, and a deferential rapport with others (Eph. 5:19-21), and whether Christ's character is evidenced in our families and on the job (Eph. 5:22-6:9).

To the extent that we are not filled with the Spirit and evidencing the character of Christ, we will of necessity be filled with a character that is contrary to that of God. "Whatever is not of faith, is sin" (Rom. 14:23). The alternative to being filled with God's character is to have "Satan fill our hearts with lying" (Acts 5:3), "rage" (Acts 19:28), "unrighteousness, wickedness, greed, evil, envy, murder, strife, deceit, and malice" (Rom. 1:29).

A second consequence of being controlled by the Spirit of Christ will be involvement in *ministry* to others. Christ's presence in us is not just for our own benefit and well-being. "God is love" (I John 4:8,16); always engaged in self-giving for the highest good of the other. Christ in the Christian will always seek to give Himself through us for others. Jesus Christ is always the Servant, and dwells in the Christian complete with all His services. He graces the Christian with spiritual giftedness (Rom. 12; I Cor. 12-14), whenever and however He sees fit to empower us for ministry. As we are filled

177

with the Spirit, we will overflow into the lives of other people, for as the Psalmist David exclaimed, "My cup overflows"
(Ps. 23:5).

The Consciousness of the Filling

How conscious will the Christian be of his being controlled by the Spirit of Christ? Should we try to ascertain how
we are doing in the process of being filled with the Spirit? Is
it any of our business to evaluate the process? If not, how do
we maintain a sense of responsibility to obey the command to
"be filled with the Spirit" (Eph. 5:18)?

Some have suggested that the objective of the Christian
life is to come to such a continual Christ-consciousness that
we think of nothing else. This is not practical. The Christian
should seek to maintain a subliminal consciousness of his
adequacy in Christ. "I can do all things through Christ who
strengthens me" (Phil. 4:13). "Our adequacy is from God" (II
Cor. 3:5), and "God is able to make all grace abound to us,
that always having all sufficiency in everything, we may have
an abundance for every good deed" (II Cor. 9:8). "We have
been granted everything pertaining to life and godliness" (II
Peter 1:3). There can be an assurance of the abundant spiritual provision we have in Jesus Christ.

The subjective consciousness of how well we are allowing for the filling of the Holy Spirit in our lives is somewhat
like the consciousness of humility. The more conscious you
are of having it, the less likely it is that you do! We must
beware of all forms of spiritual pride, and the idea that we
have "arrived" at some determined level of "spirituality."

It is more likely that the one being filled with the Holy
Spirit will be conscious and aware of his own unworthiness
and sinfulness. Like Isaiah, he will respond to the conscious-

178

ness of God's holiness by crying out, "Woe is me; I am a man of unclean lips" (Isa. 6:5). Such godly sorrow will elicit repentance and the faith which is receptive to God's activity in his life.

The consciousness of what Christ is doing in our lives is sometimes hidden from our understanding. We do not have to be conscious of what He is doing, or how well we are doing. "How unsearchable are His judgments and unfathomable his ways" (Rom. 11:33). We can be sure, though, that He is "with us always" (Matt. 28:20), and will "never desert us, or forsake us" (Heb. 13:5).

The Consummation of the Filling

When does the process of being filled and controlled by the Holy Spirit come to its intended consummation? Is a Christian ever entirely and completely filled with the Spirit while living on earth?

Though some Christians refer to an "entire sanctification" and a "complete fullness of the Spirit," Paul does not seem to claim such for himself. Writing to the Philippians, Paul explains, "Not that I have already obtained, or have already become perfect, but I press on in order that I may lay hold of that for which also I was laid hold of by Christ Jesus. I do not regard myself as having laid hold yet, but...I press on toward the goal for the prize of the upward call of God in Christ Jesus" (Phil. 3:12-14). Paul seems to indicate that as long as he is living the Christian life here on earth, he will be involved in the process of allowing for the moment-by-moment control of the Spirit of Christ in his life. As long as we are living in the here and now of earthly existence we will not arrive at some plateau where we can put our Christian life on "automatic pilot." There is a continuous responsibility for the Christian to be receptive in faith to what God wants to do in living out the life of Jesus Christ in our behavior.

Only in the heavenly realm will there be a completion of the process of being filled with the Spirit. Heaven is a place of perfection, and perfection does not allow for progression. Glorified man will still be a derivative creature, though, and will still be receptive to the controlling activity of God through him for eternity. To the extent that we now allow for the filling of the Holy Spirit we develop appreciation for the character of Christ, and a pattern of participation therein that will allow us to thus be available to the expression of His life for all eternity, unto His glory.

10

The Sanctification of Man

As the Christian individual allows the Spirit of Christ to fill and control his behavior, the divine character of holiness will be evidenced in such behavior. The presence and expression of God's holy character, whereby man functions as God created man to function, is described by the Biblical term, "sanctification."

Misconceptions abound in the minds of regenerate people as to what sanctification implies. Some picture a "sanctified saint" as a zombie-like creature walking around with a pious expression on his face – either a pasted on "evangelical smile" as if someone had just let the cat out of the bag, or a somber stare as if their best friend had just died. Others view sanctification as an ecstatic experience wherein God's blessings are dumped on an individual. A person is "zapped" by the power of God, and henceforth is as electrified and "turned on" as if they had just stuck their finger in an electric socket. Many have tended to identify sanctification with being "sanctimonious," which is laden with contemporary connotations of hypocrisy, conveying the idea of a Pharisaical piety complete with a "holier-than-thou" attitude.

The biblical meaning of sanctification needs to be understood. Paul explained to the Thessalonian Christians that "this

is the will of God, your sanctification" (I Thess. 4:3). God
has called us for the purpose of sanctification (I Thess. 4:7).
"God has chosen you from the beginning for salvation
through sanctification by the Spirit and faith in the truth" (II
Thess. 2:13). Sanctification is essential if man is to be man as
God intended man to be.

Sanctification finds its meaning in the holy character of
God. In the Hebrew language of the Old Testament the root
word *qds* meant "to cut off" or "to separate." Throughout the
Old Testament *qados* is translated "holy" and *qodes* is translated as "holiness." In the Greek language *hagos* referred to
"an object of awe" and *hages* to "that which is clean or pure."
Within the New Testament *hagios* is an adjective that is translated as "holy," *hagiotes* and *hagiosune* are translated "holiness," and *hagiasmos* is translated as "sanctification."

Two concepts are inherent in these words. First, the idea
of that which is holy, clean and pure. The second is the idea
of that which is "separate" or "set apart." The action of "setting apart" is determined by the holy character of God. Not
vice versa! Holy character is never determined by the action
of "setting apart."

In the old covenant objects and activities were referred to
as "holy" because they were "set apart" to function as the
holy God intended for His purposes. They did not possess
intrinsic holiness, but were used for divine purposes. There
were holy vessels in the holy place of the holy temple. There
were holy days and holy festivals which included the holy
Sabbath. Holy tithes were mandated. The holy scriptures
were studied. People are only rarely referred to as holy in the
Old Testament. In the new covenant literature of the New
Testament, on the other hand, the holiness of sanctification is
almost exclusively applied to people. L. S. Chafer notes that
"there is a far deeper reality indicated by (the words for holi-

ness) in the New Testament than is indicated by their employ-
ment in the Old. After all, the Old Testament is but a 'shadow
of good things to come.'"[1] Likewise, R.A. Muller explains
that "no Old Testament term is identical in significance to the
Greek New Testament word *hagiasmos*." [2]

God is Holy

The entirety of the meaning of holiness and sanctity must
be determined and defined by who God is. "I, the Lord your
God, am holy," He declares (Lev. 19:2). "I am God and not
man, the Holy One in your midst" (Hosea 11:9). By His holy
character He is set apart from all created humanity. He *does*
what He *does* because He *is* who He *is*. His activity is always
consistent with His character. The psalmist declares, "Thy
way, O God, is holy" (Ps. 77:13). God acts in a holy manner
out of His holy Being.

God is holy. This is perhaps the most comprehensive and
all-encompassing word used to describe the character of God.
R.A. Muller notes that "if a single attribute most fully
describes God in His fulness (*sic*), that attribute is holiness."[3]
To assert that "God is holy" is to explain that He is the
essence of all that is perfect (Matt. 5:48) and pure (I John
3:3). It is not that His holiness constitutes a perfect and pure
standard, but that holiness is the ontological reality of the
essence of His character. In His very Being, God is inherently
holy. He is essentially, exclusively, singularly, uniquely,
absolutely, perfectly, sovereignly, and inviolably holy!

What God is, only God is. His attributes are nontransfer-
able. To attribute an attribute of God to any created thing is to
subtly deify such. God alone is inherently and essentially
holy.

God's holy character sets Him apart from everything else. The Creator is distinguished from, separated from, distinct from all that is created. He is set apart from all that is not consistent with His character. God is set apart from all character that is impure, defiled, sinful and evil. There is a distance, a separation, from everything profane. Isaiah recognized this when he heard the seraphim declare, "Holy, Holy, Holy, is the Lord of hosts," and his own response was, "Woe is me...I am a man of unclean lips" (Isa. 6:3,5).

To note that God's holy character sets Him apart from all the created order and the sinfulness of the fallen order of mankind, does not imply a Deistic disengagement from his creation as the "wholly holy Other." God, the "Holy Father" (John 17:11), took the initiative to send the promised "Holy One" (Ps. 16:10; Acts 2:27) "in the likeness of sinful flesh" (Rom. 8:3), in order to restore man to God's intent by the indwelling presence of the Holy Spirit. Karl Barth explains that "He sanctifies the unholy by His action with and towards them, i.e., gives them a derivative and limited, but supremely real, share in His own holiness."[4]

"Be Holy as God is Holy"

Having noted that God alone is essentially and inherently holy, and that man cannot be holy in the same sense that God is holy, what is the meaning of the divine admonition to "be holy, for I am holy" (Lev. 11:44; 19:2; I Peter 1:16)?

Man is always dependent, contingent and derivative. He never has inherent or intrinsic holy character. It can never be said that "man is holy" in the same sense that we say "God is holy." The presence of holy character in man's spiritual condition and behavioral expression is always derivative. R.A. Muller states that "created things can be holy only in a derivative sense."[5] Man can never manufacture or generate holy behavior in and of himself. Devoid of the Holy Spirit by his fall into sin, man was utterly incapable of evidencing holy behavior. The old covenant admonition to "be holy, as He is holy" (Lev. 11:44; 19:2) could only serve to show that man was incapable of such.

Only when God's Holy One (John 6:69; Acts 13:35), Jesus Christ, became man and served as "a high priest, holy and undefiled" (Heb. 7:26), while also serving as the sacrificial lamb on which the death consequences of God's judgment on sin and unholiness were enacted, could the holy character of God be restored to man. This is the objective sanctification of man, whereby outside of us and within history, God acted in his Son, Jesus Christ, to sanctify mankind. Sanctification was enacted objectively and historically in the crucifixion, resurrection and Pentecostal outpouring. When Jesus exclaimed, "It is finished" (John 19:30), He was declaring the "finished work" of God whereby everything in the restored spiritual kingdom became objective reality. "Jesus gave Himself up...that He might sanctify" (Eph. 5:25,26) the new humanity of the Church. We are "sanctified through the offering of the body of Jesus" (Heb. 10:10). By "one offering" (Heb. 10:14), "through His blood" (Heb. 13:12), "the blood of the covenant, we are sanctified" (Heb. 10:29).

God's action in Jesus Christ to objectively sanctify mankind and restore His holy character to mankind, allows the divine admonition to "be holy as I am holy" (I Peter 1:16) to be invested with the divine dynamic of the activity of His holy character in man.

Holy Ones

Thus it is that the subjective sanctification within Christians can be realized by those who receive the Spirit of the Holy One, Jesus Christ, within their spirit. By the receipt of the holy presence of the Spirit of Christ, they are regarded as "Christians" and as "saints" (II Thess. 1:10) or "holy ones." This has nothing to do with the ecclesiastical canonization into sainthood within various segments of the church.

Christians are "sanctified in Christ Jesus, saints by calling" (I Cor. 1:2). By regeneration we are sanctified (I Cor. 6:11; Heb. 10:10,14), because "Christ is our sanctification" (I Cor. 1:30). Indwelt by the Holy Spirit (II Tim. 1:14), we have the "Spirit of holiness, Jesus Christ our Lord" (Rom. 1:4). "Partakers of the divine nature" (II Peter 1:4), we are "partakers of His holiness" (Heb. 12:10), and are "complete in Christ" (Col. 2:10) without deficiency in terms of our spiritual condition. By the imputed holiness of the presence of the Holy One, Jesus Christ, we are a "new man...created in holiness" (Eph. 4:24), regarded as "holy and blameless" before God (Eph. 1:4; Col. 1:22). Collectively Christians are part of the "holy priesthood" (I Peter 2:5) and the "holy nation" (I Peter 2:9) of God. This spiritual condition of Christian "holy ones" is sometimes referred to as "positional sanctification" in order to distinguish it from the "experiential sanctification" of God's holy character being manifested in behavioral expression.

Perfecting Holiness

How can holiness be perfected? Holiness is the perfection of God character, and as such is imperfectible. But the manifestation of God's holy character in Christian behavior can be progressively more representative. Thus it is that Paul encourages Christians to be "perfecting holiness in the fear of God" (II Cor. 7:1). Though made holy in subjective spiritual condition by the presence of the indwelling Holy One, Jesus Christ, Christians are still called to "be holy, as He is holy" (I Peter 1:16) in the subjective "experiential sanctification" of soul and body as well as spirit (I Thess. 5:23).

The Reformers in their reaction to the Catholic doctrine of an infusion of inherent holiness which divinized the Christian, did a real disservice to biblical theology by separating justification and sanctification in a psychologistic *ordo salutis*. Emphasizing the legal/penal model of atonement and justification, the practical impact was to diminish emphasis on holy living and the outworking of God's holy and righteous character.

God "called us with a holy calling" (II Tim. 1:9); He "called us for sanctification" (I Thess. 4:7) that we might be a people engaged in "holy conduct and godliness" (II Peter 3:11). God "disciplines us for our good, that we may share His holiness" (Heb. 12:10).

Christians are to "pursue sanctification" (Heb. 12:14), "possess their own vessel in sanctification" (I Thess. 4:4), "present their bodies as a holy sacrifice" (Rom. 12:1), and "present their members as slaves of righteousness, resulting in sanctification" (Rom. 6:19).

Such holy behavior is not just an ethical aspiration or a moral ideal. We are not sanctified by the human performance of working harder, positive thinking, dedication or commitment. The expression of holiness in man's behavior is always derived from the character and dynamic of God. If behavior is not derived from God, *ek theos*, it is not holy behavior. This is why Turner explains that "*hagiasmos* connotes the state of grace or sanctity not inherent in its subject, but the result of outside action."[6] Paul urged Christians to allow "the God of peace to sanctify you. . .He will bring it to pass" (I Thess. 5:23,24). The Christian never has inherent or self-generated holiness. The holiness of spiritual condition and behavioral expression is always derived from the holy character of God. The imputed holiness received at regeneration is imparted in our behavior by the dynamic of God in Christ.

The responsibility of the Christian is the dependency of faith, being our receptivity of God's activity. The risen Lord Jesus explained that people are "sanctified by faith in Me" (Acts 26:18). It is a "sanctification by the Spirit and faith" (II Thess.. 2:13), wherein we have a "cleansing of our hearts by faith" (Acts 15:9) and participate in a "righteousness from faith to faith" (Rom. 1:17). Christian freedom is evidenced in that we are free to exercise such faith and thus be functional humanity as God intended man to be.

Sanctification is a process. Explaining the Greek word *hagiasmos*, William Barclay notes that "all Greek nouns which end in *-asmos* describe, not a completed state, but a process. Sanctification is not a completed state; it is the road to holiness."[7] There is a subjective crisis in regeneration whereby we are made holy in spiritual condition, but henceforth we engage in the process of manifesting God's holy character in the behavior of Christian living. Writing to the Thessalonians, Paul refers to "salvation through sanctification" (II Thess. 2:13). Salvation is the process of being made safe from the dysfunction of satanic misuse and abuse, in order to function as God intended by being a vessel of His holy character. We are "being saved" (I Cor. 1:18; II Cor. 2:15) through the sanctification process. The "sanctification blob" referred to in the previous chapter (cf. pg. 172) illustrates the ever-increasing process of Christian maturity and growth in the expression of God's holy character.

As the sanctification process transpires in Christian behavior the Christian is "transformed into the same image from glory to glory" (II Cor. 3:18). The "image of God," the visibility of God's character, is expressed as God intended (Gen. 1:26,27). The "fruit of the Spirit" (Gal. 5:22,23), the "fruit of righteousness" (Phil. 1:11), reveals the character of Christ. In that process God's holy character overcomes the expression of satanic character. We are "set apart" from immorality, impurity and sin. This explains why sanctification is often contrapositioned with "defilement of flesh" (II Cor. 7:1), "sexual immorality" (I Thess. 4:3), "lustful passion" (I Thess. 4:5), "impurity" (I Thess. 4:7), and other sinful behaviors. The holy character of God supersedes diabolic character expression, and sets us apart from sin.

To what extent does such a process take place in the Christian life? Can it ever be said that a Christian is entirely sanctified? Perfectionist theology has often interpreted Paul's statement to the Thessalonians to mean that we can be "sanctified entirely. . .without blame at the coming of our Lord Jesus Christ" (I Thess. 5:23). This is usually posited as a crisis experience in a "second work of grace," denying that sanctification is a process. Elsewhere Paul explains, "Not that I have already become perfect, but I press on in order that I may lay hold of that for which also I was laid hold of by Christ Jesus" (Phil. 3:12).

The teleological implications of sanctification are referred to throughout the New Testament scriptures. The objective of God is that His holy character might be expressed in the behavior of men unto His own glory until Christ returns and unto eternity. Christians are to allow the divine dynamic of Father, Son and Holy Spirit to "establish their hearts unblameable in holiness...at the coming of our Lord Jesus" (I Thess. 3:13; 5:23). God will "perfect us until the day of Jesus

Christ" (Phil. 1:6), that we might "stand in the presence of
His glory, blameless with great joy" (Jude 1:24). The ultimate
completion of the sanctification process will come in the glorified state wherein we participate in the complete and eternal
appreciation of God's holiness.

"God has called us to sanctification. He who rejects
this...rejects God who gives His Holy Spirit to us" (I Thess.
4:7,8). To be engaged in the sanctification process is essential
and imperative. It is "the sanctification without which no one
will see the Lord" (Heb. 12:14). To manifest the holy character of God in our behavior unto His glory is the purpose for
which we exist on earth.

Religion always has the tendency to attempt to determine
holiness by emphasizing the human moral performance of
being "set apart." This is the wrong starting point. The religious Pharisees were "separated ones" who attempted to set
themselves apart by legalistic performance of the Law in
order to be holy. The early Christian ascetics attempted to set
themselves apart in monastic enclaves in order to avoid impurity and to be holy. Throughout the history of the Christian
religion there has been a misemphasis on being "set apart" by
morality codes, belief-systems, experiences, and spiritual giftedness. Setting oneself apart in separatism, isolationism,
exclusivism or elitism does not establish holiness. Such activity is merely the "works" of religion.

Christian teaching must commence with the reality of
"Christ in you" (Col. 1:27). Sanctification is the holy character of God inherent in the Holy One, Jesus Christ, via the
Holy Spirit, coming to dwell in the spirit of a believer who
will allow such holy character to be evidenced in Christian
behavior, setting him apart from impurity and sin, and setting
him apart to function as God intended. God must do the "setting apart," and He does so on the basis of His holy character,
and by the dynamic of His grace.

11

The Responsibility of Man

Emphasis upon the activity of God by His grace in order to manifest His character within His creation, necessitates an inquiry about the responsibility of man, or more specifically of the responsibility of the Christian person within the Christian life. Two extremes must be avoided. The first over-emphasizes the sovereignty of God and implies that man is incapable of responding, or has no need to respond, to God's action. Their motto is: "The Christian life is all of God." The second extreme over-emphasizes the responsibility and activity of man, indicating that the Christian life is dependent on man's commitment, dedication and performance – a theology of "works." A biblically balanced perspective of the Christian's responsibility is a necessity.

Writing to the Galatians who were being misinformed about the responsibilities of Christians, Paul asks, "Did you receive the Spirit by works of the Law, or by hearing with faith?" (Gal. 3:2). If they had listened to Paul's proclamation, they knew that "by grace you have been saved through faith; and that not of yourselves, it is the gift of God; not as a result of works, that no one should boast" (Eph. 2:8,9). In like manner as their initial response to the redemptive work of Jesus Christ, their continuing responsibilities in the Christian life were not "works of the Law," but "hearing with faith." Paul asks, "Are you going to be perfected by the flesh" (Gal. 3:3), by the works of performance? The implied answer to this rhetorical question is obviously, "No!" It is not the responsibility of Christians to be perfected and sanctified by the fallacy of self-generated activity.

When Paul later wrote to the Christians of Colossae, who were also being misled concerning the responsibilities of the Christian life, he advised them, "As you therefore have received Christ Jesus the Lord, so walk in Him" (Col. 2:6). How does anyone receive Christ Jesus the Lord? By faith! "You are all sons of God through faith in Christ Jesus" (Gal. 3:26). How, then, are we to "walk" and conduct our Christian lives? By faith! The context of Paul's statement to the Colossians evidences that he was referring to "the stability of their faith" (Col. 2:5), and their "being established in their faith" (Col. 2:7). The responsibility of man in the Christian life is faith!

What is faith? In our previous consideration of the initial faith response of man to the person and work of Jesus Christ, it was noted that faith is best defined as "our receptivity of God's activity." Initially we are receptive to the objective redemptive action of Jesus Christ on our behalf, and receptive of the subjective presence of the Spirit of Christ coming to indwell and regenerate our spirit. Henceforth, we are to be receptive to the continuing grace of God in Jesus Christ in order to behaviorally manifest His character and activity in our behavior.

The definition of faith as "our receptivity of God's activity," presupposes that God created man with the volitional capability to respond to a spiritual being. Man has a "response-ability" or an "avail-ability" to respond to spiritual activity and avail himself to such. God self-limited Himself functionally to act in correspondence with the choices of dependency, contingency and derivation that man might make, but as choosing creatures men must bear the consequences of their choices. Faith is the responsible choice of man to derive all from God. John Murray explains that "faith is not the act of God. Faith is an activity on the part of the person and of him alone. In faith we receive and rest upon Christ."[1] In recognizing that faith is man's volitional choice, careful clarification must be made in denying that such a choice has any causal significance or any meritorious benefit before God. The human choice of faith does not in any way make God contingent upon man's response.

As the Creator, God's inherent function is to act in accord with His character. The creature, man, on the other hand, is not designed with an inherent capability to act self-generatively, but is designed to function by receptivity, as a dependent, contingent and derivative creature. Our faith responses are not just mental recognition of what God has done or is doing, nor are they volitional resolutions to activate our behavior in accord with God's expectations. The response of faith is the willingness of man to be receptive to the activity of God. William Barclay noted that "the first element in faith is what we can only call receptivity."[2] This is not simply receptivity of facts; not just receptivity of the significance of the facts; but receptivity of Jesus Christ – His life and the expression of His character.

By faith we avail ourselves of the Being and activity of God. Faith is not just an epistemological assent to precepts, promises, principles or propositions. Rather, faith is an ontological receptivity of the Person of the divine "I AM." We are not merely receptive to His "message" or to His "benefits," but we are receptive to His dynamic activity of grace in His Son, Jesus Christ. God is an active God who always acts consistently with His character. He *does* what He *does* because He *is* who He *is*! We have the unique opportunity to be receptive of His active character expression in our behavior by faith.

The popular, but inadequate, definitions of faith must be replaced with a more Biblical understanding of "our receptivity of God's activity." Faith is much more than a cognitive assent to the veracity of historical and theological data. Faith is much more than subjective assurances of inner feelings of peace and well-being. Faith is much more than a willful determination to respond in moral conformity. Faith is our choice to allow God to act in and through us.

If the responsibility of the Christian is to be receptive to God's activity by faith, then what import do the hundreds of imperative verbs have which are found throughout the new covenant writings of the New Testament? What should be our response to the commands made by Jesus and by authors such as Paul, Peter and John? Are we responsible to obey the commandments of the New Testament, and if so what does such obedience entail? These are questions which must be addressed in order to understand our responsibility in the Christian life.

Dependent Attitude of Faith

Many of the imperative verbs of the New Testament command us to respond to Jesus Christ in a dependent attitude of faith. They express our responsibility as Christians to accept and develop attitudes in our mind and emotions which will serve to facilitate a volitional choice of faith in our will. Paul advises the Colossians to "set your mind on things above" (Col. 3:2), and urges the Philippians to "let your mind dwell on things which are true, honorable, right, pure, lovely and of good repute" (Phil. 4:8). Previously the Philippian Christians were told to "have this attitude (humility of mind) which was also in Christ Jesus" (Phil. 2:3-5). Some additional commands which inculcate a dependent attitude of faith include:

Reckon yourselves. Writing to the Romans, Paul exhorts the Christians to "reckon yourselves to be dead to sin, but alive to God in Christ Jesus" (Rom. 6:11). The Greek word *logizomai* was originally an accounting term. It means "to regard or consider it as a fact," "to count on it or depend on it." When we write a check we reckon on the fact that we have money which was previously deposited in the bank. The reckoning must be based upon an existent reality. Mental reckoning does not create the reality as some have fallaciously suggested. The reality on which Paul encourages us to reckon is that our prior identification as an "old man" (Rom. 6:6), wherein we were spiritually united with the satanic source of sin, has been terminated, and we are now, as Christians, spiritually united and identified with the Spirit of Christ whose inherent life (John 14:6) has been invested in us. Christians are responsible to "count it as a fact" that this is the spiritual reality within them, and to depend on the life of the risen Lord Jesus expressed in their behavior.

Submit yourselves. James, the brother of Jesus, admonishes Christians to "submit therefore to God" (James 4:7). Submission involves recognition and response to a rightful authority. In every authority structure, those who are subject to authority must learn to recognize that submission must be an attitude expressed in relational activity. The activity without the attitude is mere capitulation or resignation. In a dependent attitude of faith we submit ourselves to divine authority and to the Lordship of Jesus Christ in our lives.

Present yourselves. In the same context in which Paul explained the responsibility of Christians to "reckon themselves" (Rom. 6:11), he goes on to advocate the responsibility of "presenting ourselves." "Present yourselves to God as those alive from the dead, and your members as instruments of righteousness to God" (Rom. 6:13). "Present your members as slaves to righteousness, resulting in sanctification" (Rom. 6:19). The *King James Version* translated these verbs as "yield yourselves," which is a valid translation but tends to convey the connotation of passivity. The call to "present ourselves" seems to connote a more active responsibility of placing ourselves in the context of God's sovereign activity. Later in the same epistle Paul urges Christians "to present your bodies a living and holy sacrifice, acceptable to God, which is your spiritual service of worship" (Rom. 12:1). In a dependent attitude of faith, Christians are to "give themselves to the Lord" (II Cor. 8:5) in a voluntary sacrifice whereby we surrender ourselves to His activity in our lives.

Abide. Jesus commanded His disciples to "abide in Me, and I in you" (John 15:4). To "abide" is to remain where you are "in Him," and to "stay put." By God's grace we are put "in Christ," and we are to stay there, remain there, abide there. The English word "abode" refers to a dwelling place, such as a house where we live. Our abode is where we abide, and the ongoing responsibility to "abide" involves our residing, dwelling, living and making our residence in the context of Christ's activity. We are to "abide in Him" (I John 2:28).

Rest. The responsibility to "rest" is seldom advocated in the activistic orientation of the church and the world today. The writer to the Hebrew Christians indicates that "we who have believed enter the rest of God" (Heb. 4:3), but there is still a responsibility to "enter that rest." "Let us fear lest, while a promise remains of entering His rest, any one of you should seem to come short of it" (Heb. 4:1). "Be diligent to enter that rest" (Heb. 4:11). The background for understanding what it means to "enter God's rest" is to be found in the creation account of Genesis where God "rested" on the seventh day. It was not that God was tired and needed a rest in order to recuperate, nor that He sat back after creation with nothing more to do. He rested from His creative activity in order to enjoy that which He had created, and specifically to receive the glory from His glorious character manifested within the behavior of created humanity who were receptive to such in faith. The seventh day of each week was designated as the Sabbath, the day of rest, when men could participate in the "rest" that God was enjoying and appreciate what God was doing. After the fall of man into sin, Jesus came to restore man's participation in the "rest of God," saying "Come unto Me all who are weary and heavy-laden and I will give you *rest*. Take My yoke upon you and learn from Me, for I am gentle and humble in heart, and you shall find *rest* for your souls" (Matt. 11:28,29). In a dependent attitude of faith we participate in God's "rest" as we are receptive to the activity of Christ in us. Spirit-union allows for soul-rest.

These dependent attitudes for which we are responsible as Christians are just differing facets of faith. To "reckon" is faith counting on the reality. To "submit" is faith yielding to authority. To "present" is faith offering ourselves to the rightful owner. To "abide" is faith remaining where God puts us. To "rest" is faith enjoying God's activity. These may seem to be rather passive, but they are dependent attitudes which lead to the disciplined activities of faith.

Disciplined Activities of Faith

Other imperative admonitions in the New Testament advise the Christian to abstain from certain activities or to engage in various activities. These activities are not self-generated, but are part of the choice of faith. In choosing to be receptive to Christ's activity in our behavior, we are at the same time choosing to abstain from behavioral activity which is the satanic expression of sinfulness and selfishness, by allowing the divine activity to supersede and overcome.

The Christian is responsible to make disciplined choices to abstain or engage in various activities. Paul advised Timothy, "Discipline yourself for the purpose of godliness" (I Tim. 4:7). The Greek word *gumnazo* which Paul used is the basis of the English words "gymnasium" and "gymnastics." Discipline involves regular exercise, like an athlete preparing himself for the Olympics. For Christians such discipline in the Christian life is a structured pattern of chosen behavior that allows God to carry on His divine activity within their lives. It is the deliberate and willful placement of our being into a state, position or sphere of activity wherein God's divine objectives may be furthered and accomplished in our lives.

These disciplined activities of faith are not to be construed as "works" of performance by which we activate Christian living, or by which we earn or merit God's pleasure or benefits. They are chosen activities wherein we place ourselves in the stream of God's grace, in order to allow for the activity of His grace to express His character in the midst of the activity.

We are to "abstain from wickedness" (II Tim. 2:19), "fleshly lusts" (I Peter 2:11), "immorality" (I Thess. 4:3) and "every form of evil" (I Thess. 5:22). We are responsible to choose "not to be conformed to this world" (Rom. 12:2) and "the former lusts" (I Peter 1:14), but to "deny ungodliness and worldly desires" (Titus 2:12). Christians are to "put no confidence in the flesh" (Phil. 3:3), "make no provision for the flesh" (Rom. 13:14), and avoid "turning their freedom into an opportunity for the flesh" (Gal. 5:13). They should choose "not to think more highly of themselves than they ought to think" (Rom. 12:3), "not to exalt themselves" (Matt. 23:12), not to "live for themselves" (II Cor. 5:15), but rather to "deny themselves" (Luke 9:23).

Positively, we are to "keep ourselves chaste" (Rev. 14:4) and "unstained by the world" (James 1:27), "cleansing ourselves from all defilement of flesh and spirit" (II Cor. 7:1). We are commanded to "humble ourselves in the presence of the Lord" (James 4:10), and to "clothe ourselves with humility" (I Peter 5:5). Christians should choose to "stand firm in the Lord" (Phil 4:1; I Thess. 3:8), "in the faith" (I Cor. 16:13), and "in the will of God" (Col. 4:12). They should "conduct themselves honorably" (Heb. 13:18), "in a manner worthy of the gospel of Christ" (Phil. 1:27). To do so they will "devote themselves to prayer" (I Cor. 7:5; Col. 4:2), "drawing near to God" (James 4:8) and "to the throne of grace" (Heb. 4:16).

These are representative of the hundreds of imperatives in the New Testament that advocate disciplined activities which the Christian individual chooses to abstain from or engage in so that God's activity of grace may be functional in his behavior. The physical behavioral activities are but the contexts in which God's divine activity can express His character and ministry.

Ecclesiastical admonitions have often encouraged various activities among Christians without advising of the spiritual resource of the Lord Jesus Christ on whom we depend in the "receptivity of His activity." Many spiritually new-born

Christians, after having received the Spirit of Christ by faith, have been instructed to "go out and live like Jesus and love like Jesus," as if the responsibility of the Christian life were to imitate or mimic the example of the historical Jesus. Granted, we are to "live for the Lord" (Rom. 14:8) and "live godly in Christ Jesus" (II Tim. 3:12), but this is accomplished only as "the life of Jesus is manifested in our mortal body" (II Cor. 4:10. It is clear that we "ought to love one another" (I John 4:11), for Jesus Himself said, "This is My commandment, that you love one another, just as I loved you" (John 15:12; 13:34), but "the love of God has been poured within our hearts by the Holy Spirit who was given to us" (Rom. 5:5) and is expressed only as "the fruit of the Spirit" (Gal. 5:22). The activities of faith must not be viewed as self-generated activities apart from dependency on the energizing of God in Christ.

The responsibility of our faith activities has often been summed up in the words of the popular hymn, "Trust and Obey."[3] Faith does involve trust and dependency, but obedience should not be defined in the legal terms of keeping commandments of the Law by out best self-effort to do so. In the new covenant of Christianity, "obedience" is usually the translation of the Greek word *hupakouo,* which means "to listen under." Christian obedience is listening under God to His spiritual direction in our lives, and responding by "receptivity of His activity" in "the obedience of Christ" (II Cor. 10:5). When we understand faith and obedience as the New Testament uses the terms, we will understand our responsibility to "trust and obey," for such becomes "the obedience of faith" (Rom. 1:5; 16:26).

Diligent Application of Faith

Recognizing that our responsibility is to make choices of faith which are receptive to the activity of God in our lives, we must ever be diligent and discerning to see the practical implications of such and to avoid the abusive extremes.

A dependent attitude of faith without disciplined activities of faith can produce *passivism* and acquiescence. Some Christians have improperly decided that the Christian life is all God's responsibility and that they are not responsible for anything. They sit back, twiddle their thumbs, and expect God to do it all. James seems to have been confronting both the fallacious ideas of faith as orthodox belief and faith as passive inaction when he explained that "faith, if it has no works, is dead, by itself" (James 2:17). If faith is "our receptivity of God's activity," and there is no divine activity, then there is no faith! Faith is not just our receptivity of God's ideology or moral code, but of His active expression of His character in our behavior, for which we are responsible to consent and to make choices to be engaged therein. If there is no outworking of the activity of God, then faith has been voided and substituted with epistemology or passivism.

On the other hand, disciplined activities which are not based upon a dependent attitude of faith can become religious *performance* which is nothing more than the "wood, hay and straw" of "man's works" (I Cor. 3:12-15). Ecclesiastical explanations of Christian responsibility have often emphasized disciplined activity in a legalistic framework that fails to take into account the dependent attitude of receptivity to God's activity.

Popular misconceptions of the responsibility of the Christian include the repetitive exhortations to "be more committed to the Lord." Pledges of commitment are but promises of performance which usually fail to recognize the derivation of our activity. Nowhere in the New Testament scriptures is there a call for Christians to "commit themselves" to God or to the activities and programs of the church, but there is abundant notation that we are prone to "commit sin."

Another common admonition of Christian responsibility is the call to "serve the Lord" in "Christian service." Christians are prompted to perform by the explanation that we are "saved to serve." Indeed we do "serve" as "servants of Christ," serving as instruments of Christ's activity and as worshippers of Him, but the "service" of ecclesiastical performance is denied by Paul when he explained that God is "not served by human hands, as though He needed anything, since He Himself gives to all life and breath and all things" (Acts 17:25).

The appeal to "go out" to others in missions and evangelism has been another misused and abused call to a performance of Christian responsibility. Though we are to be available to "be witnesses" (Acts 1:8) of Jesus and to "make disciples" (Matt. 28:19), everyone is not called to go to other locations in order to do so. "As we are going" through life in the place where God has put us, we are responsible to share the life of the Lord Jesus who has become our life.

Disciplined activities which do not derive from a dependent attitude of faith are but a performance of "works" which are not pleasing to God. Such religiously "righteous deeds are like a filthy garment" (Isa. 64:6) in the sight of God. "Without faith it is impossible to please God" (Heb. 11:6).

Christians who are preoccupied with either their dependent attitude or their disciplined activities, rather than focusing on Jesus Christ and the receptivity of His life, are often full of *pride* in their particular pattern of piety. The satanic temptation to turn attention to ourselves, even to our alleged attitudes or activities of faith, serves to divert attention from Jesus Christ who is the essence of Christianity.

Some Christians seem to waver between a dependent attitude and the disciplined activities of faith, developing a *para - noia* of uncertainty as to whether they are relying upon themselves or upon the dynamic of God. "Is this what I want to do, or is this what Jesus wants to do in me?" "Is this self-motivation or Christ-motivation?" "What is the will of God for me?" If a Christian has chosen in faith to be receptive to God's activity, and this is indeed the "desire of his heart," then the Christian may take it for granted that what he is doing is God's will and expressing God's character, unless it is exposed to the contrary as a selfish motivation. This is why Augustine instructed Christians to "love God and do what you want." If the Christians loves the Lord Jesus Christ with all his heart, soul, mind and strength (Luke 10:27), he will want what God wants in his life.

Our Christian lives are to be lived in the spontaneity of trusting the life of Jesus Christ to be lived out through us. To be paralyzed with the uncertainty of paranoia preempts the faithful receptivity of God's activity. It has been said that "you can't steer a ship unless it is moving," so to avoid being "dead in the water" in our Christian lives we must take the next "step of faith" and "walk in the Spirit" (Gal. 5:16,25). If we are confident of our new identity as "Christ-ones," we can behave like who we have become by being receptive to the activity of Christ's expression of His life and character through us.

The responsibility of the Christian is faith! "In like manner as we received Christ Jesus, we are to walk in Him," by faith (Col. 2:6). We "live by faith in the Son of God" (Gal. 2:20). God never commands us to do anything, but what He provides complete sufficiency for such by His grace. He is the dynamic of His own demands! We are only responsible to be and to do what God wants to be and do in us today. Whatever behavior is not derived from the "receptivity of God's activity" is necessarily sinful. "Whatever is not of faith is sin" (Rom. 14:23), for it will inevitably express a character and activity that is not derived from God and therefore cannot be consistent with His character.

Christians are responsible to respond to God's grace with a volitional receptivity and availability of faith which allows God's activity to be expressed in their behavior – the life of Jesus to be lived out through them by the empowering of the Holy Spirit, unto the glory of God.

12

The End of Man

God is inherently eternal. What God is, only God is! Eternality is not inherent to man in any of his levels of spiritual, psychological or physical function. Since man is part of the created order, we must not posit divine attributes of the Creator God to the creature-man, else we deify the creation and engage in idolatry. Man, the creature, was designed by God, the Creator, to be a dependent, contingent and derivative being who would of necessity be receptive to spiritual being and character. The intent of God was that man would be receptive to an ontological connection and spiritual union with the Being of God Himself in order to express God's character unto His glory.

Because man is not eternal, reference can be made to "the end of man" in ways that could never be applied to the eternal God. Divine eternality does not allow for derivation of qualitative character, extension of time and relation, or termination of form, yet these are factors which must be considered concerning the "end" of man.

The Greek word for "end" is *telos,* which can refer to termination and cessation, as well as final state, and also to the goal or objective of an activity. The "end of man" will be considered in terms of man's objective of glorification, his termination of physical body, and his destiny of a final state.

The End-Objective of Glorification

The effectiveness of anything can only be determined by understanding its functional purpose and objective. Failure to apprehend the goal will allow for misdirected dysfunction. Much of mankind has not grasped his *raison d'etre,* his "reason for being." The goal is not to evolve into godhood or create a heavenly utopia on earth. Many Christians have not understood the objective of the Christian life. Lacking clear-cut objective, they concentrate on the motion by becoming involved in the programs of the institution in order to achieve trivialized projects. A fanatic was once defined as "one who having lost his direction, triples his speed." This seems appropriate to much of humanity's efforts as well as ecclesiastical endeavors.

God's objective for man, the divine "end" for man, can only be determined by the stated purpose of the divine Designer. Through Isaiah the prophet, God refers to "everyone whom I have created for My glory" (Isa. 43:7). His redemptive and restorational intent for Christians is later prophesied as being "the work of My hands, that I may be glorified" (Isa. 60:21). By creation and re-creation God has determined that His intent is to be glorified through man. This is why the Westminster Confession asks, "What is the purpose of man?" and answers the question, "The chief end of man is to glorify God and enjoy Him forever." In the vision and revelation that John saw, he records the heavenly worshippers as saying, "Worthy art Thou, our Lord and our God, to receive glory and honor and power; for Thou didst create all things, and because of Thy will they existed, and were created" (Rev. 4:11).

God is glorified when His all-glorious character of perfection, purity and holiness is manifested within His creation. He is glorified by the ontological expression of His own Being and character, not by the best efforts of man to please and appease Him. Through Isaiah, God says, "I will not give My glory to another" (Isa. 42:8); "For My own sake, for My own sake, I will act; for how can My name be profaned? And My glory I will not give to another" (Isa. 48:11). The glorification of God can only be a result of the expression of His own all-glorious character.

By the fall of man into sin the ontological presence of God in man's spirit was removed, thereby making it impossible for man to derive God's character unto His glory. "All have sinned and come short of the glory of God" (Rom. 3:23). Only by the spiritual re-creation of man in Jesus Christ is the ontological presence and activity of God restored. "This is the mystery," Paul writes, "Christ in you the hope of glory" (Col. 1:27), the confident expectation of manifesting the character of God in our behavior unto the glory of God. "By Him (Jesus Christ) is our Amen to the glory of God through us" (II Cor. 1:20).

The end-objective of man is not self-glorification in the accolades and affirmations of human performance. The Psalmist rightly said, "Not to us, O Lord, not to us, but to Thy name give glory" (Psalm 115:1). We are to "do all to the glory of God" (I Cor. 10:31), but this can be accomplished only when we derive all from Him. "For from Him and through Him and to Him are all things. To Him be the glory forever" (Rom. 11:36). Spiritual derivation determines doxological direction and destiny. Only when the origin of the activity is from God can the operative behavior achieve the objective of glorifying God.

God's objective of glorifying Himself through man is not limited to this earthly existence, but extends into the eternality which we partake of by spiritual union with His Being. In the "eternal weight of glory" (II Cor. 4:17) when we become "partakers of the glory that is to be revealed" (I Peter 5:1), we shall continue to derive God's character expression unto His glory. We shall "be glorified with Him" (Rom. 8:17) in the glorification of the final heavenly state. The end-objective of glorification continues to be man's purpose, both presently and forever. "Christ shall even now, as always, be exalted in my body, whether by life or by death" (Phil. 1:20).

The End-Termination of the Physical Body

Human physicality is not eternal. The physical body of man terminates its life function at physical death. James explains that "the body apart from the spirit is dead" (James 2:26), apparently indicating that the physical body is non-functional and non-viable at that point, and therefore terminal.

Throughout human history man has attempted to understand and explain the terminus of physical death, the phenomenon of human mortality. Some have suggested the explanation of **annihilationism**, indicating that when man dies he just passes out of existence, ceases to be, terminates into non-existence at every level of his function, spiritual, psychological and physical. There is no eternality attributed to man in annihilationism. Others have advocated the theory of **cyclicism**, whereby the physical death of man sets man free to come around again in another physical form. Such theories of the transmigration of the soul and reincarnation presuppose an eternality of soul and spirit that is cyclically embodied in a sequence of temporal physical forms. The explanation of **Christian religion** has sometimes been based on the alleged eternality of the physical body which will be resurrected and restored in the heavenly realm, as well as an inherent eternality of soul and spirit whereby all men allegedly will live forever either in heaven or in hell. A more **scriptural explanation** is to recognize that there is no inherent eternality to man in spirit, soul or body. Man was created as a contingent and derivative creature who derives his nature and identity from spiritual solidarity with either God or Satan, which extends in a perpetuity of that connective identification to another environmental context, another realm, after physical death. Physical death then involves a discontinuity of bodily form, but a continuity of spiritual connectivity and derivation.

Divine life is eternal and cannot be terminated. Such spiritual life is made available to man in Jesus Christ. Jesus Christ is eternal life. "I am the way, the truth and the life" (John 14:6). "God has given us eternal life, and this life is in His Son. He who has the Son has the life; he who does not have the Son of God does not have the life" (I John 5:11,12); and "you may know that you have eternal life" (I John 5:13). Despite the tombstones that read, "So and so departed into eternal life on such and such a date," eternal life is not a commodity or state of existence that is dispensed after physical death. Eternal life becomes functional in an individual when he receives the life of Jesus by faith at regeneration. Jesus said, "God so loved the world that He gave His only begotten Son, that whoever believes in Him shall have eternal life" (John 3:16). "He who believes Him who sent Me has eternal life, and has passed out of death into life" (John 5:24). "He who believes has eternal life" (John 6:47). "Believing you may have life in His name" (John 20:31).

The continuity of the eternal life that we have received in Christ Jesus is assured. Jesus said, "He who believes in Me shall live even if he dies, and everyone who lives and believes in Me shall never die" (John 11:25,26). Paul explained to the Colossians that "your life is hidden with Christ in God. . .Christ is our life. . .and you will be revealed with Him in glory" (Col. 3:3,4). There is a continuity of spiritual life-content in Jesus Christ.

There is also a continuity of embodiment. When the physical body dies we do not become disembodied spirits. We "shall not be found naked" (II Cor. 5:3) without bodily covering, but will "put on the imperishable and immortal" (I Cor. 15:53,54) body. We will not be left homeless, for though we "lay aside the earthly dwelling" (II Peter 1:14) and "the earthly tent is torn down; we have a house not made with hands, eternal in the heavens" and "will be clothed with our dwelling from heaven" (II Cor. 5:1,2). We will continue to have bodily expression.

The discontinuity effected at physical death is in the context and form of our bodily expression. Paul took pains to correct the mistaken Jewish emphases on physicality. Those Jews who believed in bodily resurrection conceived of such in terms of the reconstruction and reanimation of corpses, the reactivation of distinctively Jewish physical bodies in a future nationalistic kingdom-community. In the fifteenth chapter of First Corinthians, Paul explains the discontinuity between a fleshly body and a glorified body (15:39,43), between an earthly body and a heavenly body (15:40), between a perishable body and an imperishable body (15:42,53,54), between a body of dishonor and a body of glory (15:43; Phil. 3:21), between a body of weakness and a body of power (15:43), between a natural body and a spiritual body (15:44,46), between a mortal body and an immortal body (15:53,54). This discontinuity of bodily form and feature corresponds with the discontinuity of environmental context in which those bodies function, changing from the earthly context to the heavenly context (15:46-49).

When our physical bodies come to their terminal end at physical death, that body is then disposed of by burial, cremation, or otherwise. The Spirit-permeated soul then passes from that body to be embodied with a resurrected and transformed body in the heavenly realm. Though there is the discontinuity of bodily form and contextual realm, there is a transitional continuity of spiritual life within embodiment. This "graduation to glory" is preferable in many ways to the present earthly existence, for we are free from the limitations, hindrances and encumbrances of man's fall into sin. "We are set free from the slavery to corruption into the freedom of the glory of the children of God" (Rom. 8:21). This is why Paul could declare that it was his "desire to depart to be with Christ, for that is very much better" (Phil. 1:23), to be "absent from the body and to be at home with the Lord" (II Cor. 5:8). "For me to live is Christ," Paul exclaimed in recognition of the spiritual continuity of Christ's life, and "to die is gain" (Phil. 1:21) for the discontinuity of bodily form and environmental context is indeed preferable.

The End-Destiny of the Final State

The living God is inherently and essentially life. "The Father has life in Himself" (John 5:26). He is the source of all life, for "He gives life to all" (Neh. 9:6) living things. Being Spirit (John 4:24) and eternal (Rom. 16:26), His life is spiritual life and eternal life. As such He is immortal (I Tim.

1:17); He experiences no death; and "He alone possesses immortality" (I Tim. 6:16).

Man, on the other hand, is contingent upon a spiritual being and source for his identity and existence. Man is not independent and autonomous, but dependent on an ontic-identification with either God or Satan.

The teaching of Christian religion has often accepted the Platonic premise that man has an inherently immortal soul which lives forever (eternally), and will go to one place or the other, to heaven or to hell after physical death. Many theological writers have attempted to expose the fallacy of this teaching:

> "This widely-accepted idea (of the immortality of the soul) is one of the greatest misunderstandings of Christianity."[1]

> "Our traditional thinking about the 'never-dying soul,' which owes so much to Graeco-Roman heritage, makes it difficult for us to appreciate Paul's point of view."[2]

> "the heresy about man's immortal soul ...is one of those doctrines that have been inherited by the Church from Platonic philosophy, that has simply been received without criticism and without being judged in the light of Scripture. No man is by nature immortal, either as to body or soul. Immortality is the word that can be applied only to the state of the glorified saints in Christ."[3]

God alone is essentially immortal. "God alone possesses immortality" (I Tim. 6:16). Man can only derive immortality from God, for "all immortality except God's is derived."[4] "Christ Jesus abolished death and brought life and immortality to light through the gospel" (II Tim. 1:10). The Christian derives immortality and eternal life from the essence of

Christ's life ontologically present and active within his spirit, soul and body. The continuum of that immortal, non-dying, eternal life functioning within man after his physical death is the end-destiny of the heavenly realm.

Popular religious concepts of heaven have often been ethereal cosmomorphisms of clouds, angels, harps and pearly gates. Finite human thought fixes on such figures to provide some form to spiritual abstraction; "things which eye has not seen and ear has not heard, and which has not entered the heart of man, all that God has prepared for those who love Him" (I Cor. 2:9). The danger is that these figures can become conceptual idols concretized in religious dogma. For this reason Jewish religion has usually refrained from speculating about heaven, lest it lead to forbidden idolatry.

Even the conceptualization of heaven as a "place," a localized entity which for finite minds demands space/time parameters, may be but another inadequate attempt of man to fit heaven into human formulation. If heaven is infinite and eternal, then does such allow for localization within space and time? Jesus did tell His disciples that He was "going to prepare a place for them" (John 14:2,3), but a dwelling-place "near to the heart of God" does not necessarily demand localization.

Jesus Christ is the eternal and spiritual life of God. We have received His life in regeneration. His eternal and immortal life remains in continuity beyond our physical death. Heaven is the eternal continuum of the eternal life of Jesus Christ which we now have as Christians which "shall never die" (John 11:26). Heaven is the presence of the perfect life of Jesus in an environmental context free from all imperfection and hindrance. Jesus prayed for Christians, "Father, I desire that they be with Me where I am, in order that they may behold My glory" (John 17:24). Heaven is the perpetuity of the ontic-expression of the life of Jesus Christ. "Whom have I in heaven but Thee? And besides Thee, I desire nothing on earth" (Psalm 73:25).

Hell, on the other hand, is the continuity and perpetuity of spiritual identification and union with the being and destiny of the devil. When physical death occurs in man while in a state of spiritual death, such spiritual identification with "the spirit that works in the sons of disobedience" (Eph. 2:2) will be perpetuated after the judgment in everlasting death. Such death should not be defined as termination, cessation or annihilationism, but as the absence of the presence and quality of God's life in Jesus Christ. The quantitative and qualitative perpetuity of spiritual derivation from Satan will be most unpleasant "in the everlasting fire which has been prepared for the devil and his angels" (Matt. 25:41), agents and messengers.

Understanding of the continuity and perpetuity of spiritual identification with either God or Satan in the end-destiny of our final state should serve to remove some of the crassly materialistic and mercenary expectations that some Christians have concerning the future heavenly state. Keying off of biblical statements of treasures in heaven (Matt. 19:21; Mk. 10:21; Lk. 12:21; 18:22); rewards in heaven (Matt. 10:41,42; Lk. 6:23,35; I Cor. 3:8); crowns (II Tim. 4:8; James 1:12; I Pet. 5:4; Rev. 2:10); and mansions (John 14:2-KJV), self-concerns have tainted and polluted many Christians' understanding of the heavenly reality. Many seem to think that they are going to get something more, in addition to what they already have spiritually, when they get to heaven. Although Paul does indicate that "to die is gain" (Phil. 1:21), this does not imply that we will receive something more than we already have in Jesus Christ. To suggest that more is to be "gained" is to suggest that what we have received in Jesus Christ is limited or insufficient. God forbid! "All things belong to us in Christ, things present or things to come" (I Cor. 3:21-23). "God has blessed us with every spiritual blessing in the heavenly places in Christ" (Eph. 1:3). We "have been made complete" in Christ (Col. 2:10). The "gain" that Paul refers to is not something in addition to Jesus' life, but is the discontinuity of bodily form which replaces the hindrances of physicality with the unencumbered glorified body, and the "gain" of a contextual environment to express Christ's life and character without antagonism or constraint.

The "treasures in heaven" are all inherent in the spiritual "treasure" of Christ's life that now indwells our "earthen vessels" (II Cor. 4:7). The "crown" is the victory wreath (Greek word *stephanos*), the "crown of life" (Rev. 2:10), indicating participation as "overcomers" in the victory of the Lord Jesus Christ. The "mansions" are but spiritual "dwelling places" (John 14:2) in the presence of God. "Rewards in heaven" are not additional acquisitions, for there is nothing more than "the reward of the inheritance" (Col. 3:24) of the eternal life of Jesus Christ (cf. Heb. 11:26).

When Christians display a languid and listless approach to their Christian life here on earth, longing for the future heavenly state where they expect to gain complete spirituality and full progress unto perfection, I am tempted to respond, "I don't think you are going to like heaven when you get there!" "What do you mean?" they might reply. My explanation would be, "If you do not appreciate and enjoy the life that you have in Jesus Christ right now, what makes you think you will appreciate and enjoy the continuum of that same spiritual and eternal life in Jesus Christ throughout the eternal heavenly existence?" Progress in the development of such appreciation and expression of Christ's life must take place in our present Christian lives, for there is no Biblical basis for

215

expecting further spiritual progression beyond this life. Heaven is the perfect presence of the life of God in Jesus Christ, and that which is perfect allows for no progress or development in perfection. Progression is alien to the concept of heaven. Progress is only required when things are imperfect, and is the unique quest of man after the fall. Robert Browning wrote,

"Progress is man's distinctive mark alone –
Not God's, and not the beast's;
God is, they are,
Man partly is, and wholly hopes to be."[5]

"Now is the day of salvation" (II Cor. 6:2), for progression and growth in spiritual awareness and appreciation of the life of Jesus. The extent of our capability for appreciation and expression of the divine life is developed in the present. As we are "being saved" (I Cor. 1:18), being "filled with the Spirit" (Eph. 5:18), and "growing in the grace and knowledge of our Lord and Savior Jesus Christ" (II Peter 3:18), we are developing such appreciation. Our present availability to the life of Jesus Christ allows for a greater capability of appreciation, and such is the "greater reward" of one Christian over another. All competitive and comparative elements will be eliminated, though, and there will be no envy or dissatisfaction. All Christians will see Jesus (I Cor. 13:12), glorify God, and enjoy Him forever. Everyone will be completely satisfied with the fullness of joy they have in Jesus Christ, but some will have developed a greater capacity to enjoy and appreciate the eternal life of Jesus, while no one else will know or care. All will be filled full to the extent that they are capable to glorify God forever.

Such is the "end" of "man as God intended man to be!"

ENDNOTES

2

The Constitution of Man

1   Green, Jay P. Sr., *The Interlinear Bible.* Grand Rapids: Baker Book House. 1983. pg. 1.
2   Green, Jay P. Sr., *Ibid.* pg. 1.
3   Green, Jay P. Sr., *Ibid.* pg. 2. (See also column note in *New American Standard Bible.* Lockman Foundation)
4   Green, Jay P. Sr., *Ibid.* pg. 2.

4

The Natural Man

1   Pascal, Blaise, *Provincial Letters. Great Books of the Western World.* Chicago: University of Chicago Press. 1952. Vol. 33, pg. 116.
2   Calvin, John, *Commentary on the First Book of Moses called Genesis.* Grand Rapids: Baker Book House. 1979. pg. 127.
3   Calvin, John, *Institutes of the Christian Religion.* London: James Clarke and Co. 1949. Book 1, pgs. 154,155.
4   Calvin, John, *The Gospel According to St. John.* Grand Rapids: Wm. B. Eerdmans Pub. Co. 1993. pg. 227.
5   Gerhart, Emanuel V., *Institutes of the Christian Religion.* New York: Funk and Wagnalls Co. 1894. Vol. I, pg. 697.
6   Pieper, Francis, *Christian Dogmatics.* St. Louis: Concordia Pub. House. 1957. Vol. I, pg. 509.
7   Pieper, Francis, *Ibid.* pg. 533.

8 Pieper, Francis, *Ibid.* pg. 569.

9 Cooke, William, *Christian Theology*. London: Hamilton, Adams, and Co. 1863. pg. 632.

10 Bancroft, E.H., *Elemental Theology*. Grand Rapids: Zondervan Pub. House. 1977. pg. 242.

11 Strong, Augustus H., *Systematic Theology*. Valley Forge: Judson Press. 1907. pg. 588.

12 Pink, A.W., *Gleanings in Genesis*. Chicago: Moody Press. 1981. pg. 34.

13 Pink, A.W., *Gleanings From the Scriptures*. Chicago: Moody Press. 1977. pg. 95.

14 Pink, A.W., *Ibid.* pg. 102.

15 Chafer, Louis Sperry, *Systematic Theology*. Dallas: Dallas Seminary Press. 1983. Vol. 2, pg. 99.

16 Chafer, Louis Sperry, *Ibid.*, pg. 250.

17 Chafer, Louis Sperry, *Ibid.*, pgs. 323,324.

18 Chafer, Louis Sperry, *Satan: His Motives and Methods*. Grand Rapids: Zondervan Pub. House. 1977. pg. 45.

19 Fuller, Daniel P., *International Standard Bible Encyclopedia,* article on "Satan." Grand Rapids: Wm. B. Eerdmans Pub. Co., 1988. Vol. 4, pg. 342.

20 Bell, L. Nelson, "Christianity Today" magazine, March 31, 1972.

21 Hunt, Dave, *The Seduction of Christianity*. Eugene: Harvest House Pub. 1985. pg. 118.

22 Barnett, Paul, *The Message of Second Corinthians*. Downers Grove: Inter-Varsity Press. 1988. pg. 82.

23 Kelfer, Russell, "Decisions, Decisions, Decisions." Tape #907.

24 Thomas, W. Ian, *The Mystery of Godliness*. Grand Rapids: Zondervan Pub. House. 1964. pg. 81.

25 Thomas, W. Ian, *Ibid.* pgs. 82,83.

26 Thomas, W. Ian, *Ibid.* pg. 86.

27 Thomas, W. Ian, *Ibid.* pg. 87.

5

The Perfect Man

1   Thomas, W. Ian, *The Mystery of Godliness*. Grand Rapids: Zondervan Publishing Co. 1964. Pgs. 48,49.
2   See explanation of death consequences in the chapter entitled *"The Fall of Man."*

7

The Response of Man

1   Moffatt, James, *Grace in the New Testament*. London: Hodder and Stoughton. 1931. pg. 12.
2   Thomas, W. Ian, *The Mystery of Godliness*. Grand Rapids: Zondervan Publishing House. 1964. pg. 128.
3   Thomas, W. Ian, *Ibid.* pg. 127.
4   Smedes, Lewis, *International Standard Bible Encyclopedia* (revised edition), article on "Grace." Grand Rapids: Wm. B. Eerdmans Pub. Co. Vol. 2. pg. 551.
5   Barclay, William, *The Mind of St. Paul*. London: Fontana Books. 1965. pg. 112.
6   Calvin, John, *Institutes of the Christian Religion*. London: James Clarke and Co. 1949. Book I.
7   Moffatt, James, *Op. cit.* pg. 132.
8   Thomas, W. Ian, *Op. cit.* pg. 50.
9   Berkouwer, G.C., *Faith and Justification*. Grand Rapids: Wm. B. Eerdmans Pub. Co. 1954. pg. 179.
10 Murray, John, *Redemption – Accomplished and Applied*. Grand Rapids: Wm. B. Eerdmans Pub. Co. 1978. pg. 106.

11 Bultmann, Rudolph, *The Dictionary of New Testament Theology*. Article on "faith" (*pistis*). Grand Rapids: Wm. B. Eerdmans Pub. Co. 1968. Vol. 6, pg. 219.

12 Thomas, W. Ian, from transcription of audio-taped message.

10

The Sanctification of Man

1 Chafer, Louis Sperry, *Systematic Theology,* Dallas: Dallas Seminary Press. 1983. Vol. 7. pg. 279.

2 Muller, R.A., *The International Standard Bible Encyclopedia*. Article on "sanctification." Grand Rapids: Eerdmans. 1979. Vol. 4, pg. 321.

3 Muller, R.A., *Ibid.* pg. 321.

4 Barth, Karl, *Church Dogmatics: The Doctrine of Reconciliation.* Edinburgh: T & T Clark. 1958. Vol. IV, part 2, pg. 500.

5 Muller, R.A., *op cit.* pg. 321.

6 Turner, G.A., *The Zondervan Pictorial Bible Encyclopedia.* Article on "sanctification." Grand Rapids: Zondervan Publishing House. 1977. Vol. 5, pg. 265.

7 Barclay, William, *The Letter to the Romans.* Daily Study Bible series. Philadelphia: The Westminster Press. 1957. pgs. 92,93.

11

The Responsibility of Man

1 Murray, John, *Redemption – Accomplished and Applied.*
Grand Rapids: Wm. B. Eerdmans Publishing Co. 1955. pg.
106.
2 Barclay, William, *The Mind of Paul.* London: Fontana
Books. 1958. pg. 112.
3 Sammis, John H., "Trust and Obey."

12

The End of Man

1 Cullman, Oscar, *Immortality of the Soul or Resurrection of
the Dead.* New York: Macmillan Co. 1964. pg. 15.
2 Bruce, F.F., *Paul: Apostle of the Heart Set Free.* Grand
Rapids: Wm. B. Eerdmans Pub. Co. 1977. pg. 311.
3 Hoeksema, Herman, *In the Midst of Death.* Grand Rapids:
Wm. B. Eerdmans Pub. Co. 1943. pg. 97.
4 Bruce, F.F., in the foreword to *The Fire That Consumes* by
Edward W. Fudge. Houston: Providential Press. 1982. pg.
vii.
5 Browning, Robert, "A Death in the Desert." 1864.

Glossary of Terms

anthropological - The Greek word for "man" is *anthropos*. That which is "anthropological" pertains to created mankind. The "anthropological perspective" of this book is the attempt to ascertain what it means to be "man as God intended."

epistemological - Two Greek words, *epi* meaning "upon," and *histemi* meaning "to stand," are conjoined to form the root of the word, "epistemology." Epistemology refers to the process of "taking one's stand upon" particular evidence or data, in order to determine what we believe. Why do we believe what we believe? What is the basis of our belief? Christianity is not simply a propositional belief-system, but the ontological presence and function of the Being of God in Christ Jesus.

eschatological - The Greek word *eschatos* refers to "last things." These are not just "end-times" phenomena or future events, but are the "last" in the sequence of what God has done for mankind. Jesus is the *Eschatos* man (cf. I Cor. 15:45), God's "last Word" for mankind. We live in the last era, time, day, age (cf. Acts 2:17; Heb. 1:2; I Peter 1:20), when the risen and living Lord Jesus is available to indwell receptive individuals.

ontological - The Greek word *ontos* refers to "being." God alone has inherent, essential Being, and all of the created order has "being" derived out of (*ek*) God's Being. All Christian theology must begin with consideration of the Being and character of God. God *does* what He *does*, because He *is* Who He *is*. His every action is energized out of His own Being. The Christian life is not to be viewed as a separated or deistic attempt to please God or live like Jesus. The very Being of God by the presence of the Spirit of the living Lord Jesus must be present and functioning in the receptive Christian individual in order to have Christian life.

When the word "ontological" is used in this work (as it often is), there is an underlying presupposition of the necessity of spirit-being (either God or Satan) operating within derivative mankind. Evil character is derived from the being of the Evil One. The Being of God in Jesus Christ must be present and functioning in a receptive Christian for "man to be man as God intended."

theodicy - a philosophical and theological term that refers to an explanation of the source of evil and all that is contrary to God's character. Identifying the source of evil has long been an enigma in Christian thought. This book accepts the earliest Christian premise that evil is derived from the Evil One, Satan. How and why Lucifer became the devil, the originator and facilitating source of evil, remains an enigma.

thanatological - The primary Greek word for "death" is *thanatos*. The word "thanatological" is used in this work to refer to the various processes of death that became operative in the human race because of the sin of Adam. "The devil, the one having the power of death" (cf. Heb. 2:14) was henceforth present and operative in unregenerate mankind. Jesus Christ incurred the death consequences that occurred in Adam, to deliver mankind from the stranglehold of death and make available God's life, His own life, to those who would receive Him.

Made in the USA
Lexington, KY
27 August 2011